When Work is Good

When Work is Good

What it Means
Why it Drives Results
How You Can Build a Workplace People Love

A 2ND edition, re-rendered, of **BRAVESPACE WORKPLACE:**
MAKING YOUR COMPANY FIT FOR HUMAN LIFE

Moe Carrick

Printed in the United States of America
First Printing, 2023

ISBN: 979-8-9886390-0-8
Library of Congress Control Number: 2023913561

Moementum Press
www.moementum.com

Dedication

This book is dedicated to the People Leaders out there—you are central to making work good. People know their organization through you, and their entire experience is shaped by their relationship with you. Remember that, more than anything else, people need and want you to show up authentically with both your gifts and your flaws. You are enough.

And to workers everywhere, the employees at the front line who do the things that must be done at workplaces large and small. You are the heart of it all, and what you do every day makes your company great. Remember that meaningful work is vital to life, and the two are intertwined. Hold fast to being brave, even when it feels hard, because your thriving at work matters to you, your family, your community, and your organization.

Contents

Foreword

I went to Harvard Business School in the late 80s. We were taught that leaders were strong and decisive, that they dressed and spoke with confidence, and knew how to work a room to achieve their goals. We were taught to be rigorous with our analysis and to always deliver on our commitments. We learned how to navigate financial statements and organizational charts and marketing plans. I remember so many cases and courses and discussions about how to be successful, but I can't recall a single conversation about how or why I might need to be brave. From the perspective of time, however, I see that many of my best moments as an employee and as a leader involved courage. Courage required me to push beyond my comfort zone—taking an assignment I wasn't fully prepared for or deviating from the typical linear career path. Stepping away from a cushy headquarters job to go out to the field and sell. Moving my family across the country for a radical career change. Letting go of a high-performing employee who was creating a toxic work environment. These decisions all took courage. And while they didn't all go as planned, each brave decision showed me the value of navigating by my success criteria and not conventional wisdom.

Sometimes bravery involved speaking truth to power, which was especially challenging as a female leader in male-dominated situations.

Many times, bravery involved how I showed up for my team. Learning the paradox of confidence and humility required me to admit when I didn't know the answer or had made a mistake. Learning that great teams happen when I hire people who are better than me, not people I can control. Having the difficult conversations that require both radical candor and care when someone isn't performing or is in the wrong job.

It's hard work to be a brave leader. I have failed more times than I have succeeded. It's so much easier to retreat behind your spreadsheet than to dive into the messy, difficult business of people's hearts. Early in my career, I took a Myers-Briggs personality assessment that pegged me as a natural Feeler (F) who had trained herself to be a Thinker (T). My coach counseled that that's a difficult place to be—to know that many work situations require you to lead with objectivity and rationality and to prioritize logic over emotions, while at heart being deeply empathetic to the human factors involved in decisions. At the time I dismissed her comments and took pride in the fact that I had learned to shape myself in the mold of the more typical business leader.

Now I see it differently. The world needs brave leaders who understand that bringing their heart to work doesn't mean they're weak, don't care about results, or don't have what it takes to make tough decisions.

As Moe points out, "People are what make companies great," and employees today have more choices than ever—if they don't like their boss or work environment, they'll leave to find another. And even if they don't leave, they surely won't give their full effort to an employer that they see as unaware or unempathetic to the realities of life's messiness. As leaders, how do we create an environment where employees can thrive and contribute fully to the success of their organizations?

Simply put, we must commit to creating the conditions that allow employees to bring their best selves to work. We can pursue what Moe calls Bravespace workplaces. For the young manager, this might mean taking the time to get to know her direct reports and being honest about her own limitations and fears. (I still remember how demoralized I was by a first time boss who felt she needed to assert her power by micromanaging me, even though she only had one more year of experience than me.) For the head of a department, it might mean actively creating a shared sense of purpose by thinking as deeply about the team dynamics as he does about managing each individual. For an executive, it might mean boldly pursuing policies such as flexible work hours or paternity leave to help reduce employees' stress stemming from family commitments.

As leaders, we have the opportunity and responsibility to show up with courage and conviction. We each have the opportunity to develop both the heart and the head that we bring to our work.

When I reflect on the leaders who have drawn out my best work, I realize that they're the ones who have shown me that I was seen and cared for. They didn't shy away from giving me tough feedback, and certainly didn't accept shoddy efforts or poor results. But those actions aren't the ones that carried the biggest impact. What I hold sacred is the memory of the boss who flew across the country to attend my dad's funeral. The boss who bought me a bottle of champagne when I completed a particularly onerous project. The boss who said yes to a part-time arrangement when I wanted to help my husband start a business. These actions brought out my best self. These leaders taught me to be brave.

I am fortunate that what I didn't learn about courage and heart from business school I was able to learn from these wise bosses and from my own successes and failures. But I so wish I had had Moe's book.

I envy the young manager about to dive into the pages ahead. You can learn so much that will positively impact you and the people you'll go on to lead. I feel kinship with those of you of my vintage. Our age frees us from some of the fears about our careers and allows us to speak up about what we believe to be right.

Moe's book gives us data and techniques that we can use to positively change broken systems.

Together we can change workplaces and make them actually good for the people who inhabit them. Together we can create the bravespaces that will improve our businesses, our communities, and the world.

—**Cammie Dunaway,** former CMO, Duolingo,
Co-Author with Moe Carrick of best-selling book
FIT Matters: How to Love Your Job

Acknowledgments

The experience of working with clients these past 30 years is at the core of my learning, and I'm grateful and humbled by the privilege of working with every single one of you. You have opened your companies to me, invited me into your innermost fears, and shared your legacy dreams. It's a privilege and an honor to work beside you.

Globally, millions of employees come to work day in and day out, counting on you to provide good work for them, to help them grow, and to enable the health and success of their families and communities.

Watching you lead your organizations gives me hope for our collective future. Thank you.

I appreciate the social justice and education leaders (Brian Arao and Kristi Clemens, Diana Ali, et al.) who first coined the term bravespace as an alternative to *safe space* when describing how college campuses protect and support freedom of expression. I had used the term *bravespace* to define the workplaces I felt were necessary for business tomorrow before I learned of the term's use in the university context. While the context is different for Bravespace workplaces, the meaning is adjacent and aligned. Thank you for your work.

Huge shout-outs to my agent, Kelli Christianson, for your unwavering faith in me, your patience, your honest feedback, and the delight of partnership. To my editors, Cameron

Carrick, Lieve Maas, and Julie Swearingen, your critical eye, challenging questions, endless compassion, and inquisitive minds were assets in every stage of writing, especially the last one, where we wrestled the book down to its essence.

To my incredible team at Moementum, Inc., family and friends, thank you for understanding and patiently loving me through research, writer's block, editing binges, and self-criticism, even while I missed precious time with you in order to birth *the book*.

To Jim, thank you for being on this wild ride.

Thank you to my children for always keeping it real and teaching me everything I know that counts. The future is in good hands with you, and you each inspire me daily.

Prologue:
Canary in a Coal Mine

Don't save the canary. Fix the mine.

—Seth Godin

My second book, *Bravespace Workplace: Making Your Company Fit for Human Life*, was published in October 2019 by Maven House Press. It represented years of research and consulting with organizations, and I felt excited and proud to see it manifest in the world.

I had that burning in my chest feeling that the world needed to know what was happening in most workplaces globally, quietly simmering beneath the surface of productivity and return for investors: Work wasn't working.

And even worse, if we didn't fix it, we stood to lose individual and collective wealth, health, and social stability. The consequences were enormous on economic, personal, community, and family health.

At the same time, I felt impotent, unseen, and small.

Other voices crowded the space of business publishing, and my experience and findings felt drowned out by the roar of pundits, academics, and gurus all trying to get a piece of the multi-billion dollar industry that is "leadership."

I felt a deep affinity with the tiny, soft, yellow canaries that accompanied miners as they have traveled for centuries deep into the lightless, cold earth to extract iron ore. Until 1986, canaries were brought into the mines because when the air got toxic from carbon monoxide fumes, the birds died first, warning miners of the deadly gases that would soon take their lives if they didn't leave.

I felt like I was singing at the top of my lungs for organizational leaders, employees, business owners, shareholders, and boards to notice and believe me, but despite my loyal clients and followers, the book landed with acclaim but only a small ripple of a splash.

I stayed focused anyway, busy working with clients who were listening and noticing, and it felt energizing and hopeful to work with leaders who cared about and wanted to build highly valued organizations by highly valuing their people.

A mere three months after the book's release, I returned from work with a client in Scotland and commented to my husband that the flu must be bad because many more people than usual were wearing masks in the airport.

Enter Coronavirus disease, aka COVID-19, caused by the SARS-CoV-2 virus.

The entire world shut down, everyone that could stayed home, and workplaces changed forever.

Like many, I thought quarantine would last a few weeks or at most, a few months. How wrong I was.

March 20, 2020, was the day I admitted to myself that my business was irrevocably changed, and the last three years have been an endless series of unexpected roller-coaster turns for all of us. Each has made us lurch and revealed a dizzying array of previously unconsidered realities.

- Toilet paper shortages as people hoarded theirs.
- People being sent home to work.
- Schools closing and then moving teaching to virtual.
- Offices re-opening, then re-closing, often forever.
- Travelling nurses coming to the aid of front-line healthcare, unwittingly contributing to financial ruin for many systems.
- Zoom and Teams becoming household words for us all.
- Backdrop becoming a thing.

And, for the purposes of this book, the world of work is being seen in a whole new light. There are even new words and terms that didn't exist before the world shut down:

- The Great Resignation
- Contactless
- Quiet Quitting
- Essential Worker
- Elbow Bump
- Zoom Fatigue
- PPE
- Quaranteam

- Hybrid Workplace
- Social Distancing
- WFH (Work From Home)

Additionally, several powerful research studies emerged during the three years since my book, *Bravespace Workplace*, was first released that underlined and put a giant exclamation point on my message. More about these studies in later chapters, but suffice it to say, I am indebted to the research of the McKinsey Global Survey,[1] the COVID-19 Work and Health Survey, Gartner's Future of Work After COVID-19 Study,[2] Deloitte's Report on Workplace Well-Being, The Surgeon General's Report[3] "Workplace Well-Being and Mental Health," and others for bringing proof to what many of us already knew.

This canary feels seen and heard.

The whole world is now listening to the fact that our collective well-being at work is essential to both business results and the overall health of our future societies.

And those who aren't listening should be.

And yet, I am troubled by the persistent belief that the issues we face with workplaces today are new and arose singularly out of the COVID-19 crisis. Why have we consistently known that life-centeredness mattered at work but failed to effectively create solutions to broken workplace cultures, employees who take the role of victims, and leaders who are bad for people?

In a podcast together, Brené Brown, Adam Grant, and Simon Sinek, all renowned academics in the realm of organizational leadership, spoke about the pendulum of management fads starting in the industrial revolution, covering the Hawthorne experiences of the 1920s, and movements in the 1960s about meaningful work, followed by a backslide taking us into the present.

We have had compelling data points but were unable or unwilling to muster collective action that changed things substantively. What strikes me is this: because we didn't want to believe that workplaces were failing, we did not pay attention until we could no longer avoid the reality that they were.

This is why I decided to release a second edition of my 2nd book, *Bravespace Workplace: Making Your Company Fit for Human Life,* with updated research, a clarified model, and a new title.

The canaries in the metaphoric coal mines of workplaces have been both, literally and figuratively, dying because of toxic leaders, their own passivity, unsafe cultures, and work-related stress and trauma for a long, long time.

My biggest fear is that the last three years of burgeoning awareness of the problem simmers back down after a temporary uptick to a complacent and comfortable return to work as we have always known it.

Failing to learn from what we have learned about workplace health in 2020-2022 would be a travesty.

The impact could be the most dire for young workers just starting their careers. How can they be expected to bring their talents, their energy, their bright ideas, and their time to jobs that suck the life out of them or even worse, cause permanent harm?

People of my vintage (Baby Boomers and Gen X) may tell ourselves the story that we made it through the gauntlet of hostile working conditions, so why can't young people? The implications of this mindset is that young workers just need to "toughen up."

I maintain that we did not survive without consequence. Almost every person I have worked with over the past 30 years (and the number is in the tens of thousands) has a story of workplace trauma that they have had to recover from, including me.

I have endured bosses who wanted to flirt with me (or worse) and expected me to just assume that tolerating their advances was an expectation of the job, companies that asked me to hide evidence that I had children, blatantly unequal pay for equal work, leaders who publicly humiliated me, co-workers who lied and threw me under the bus, and more, as have most of you.

The costs of the toxicity we have collectively endured at work are enormous.

COVID-19 and the whole world shutting down gave us an unprecedented wake-up call to actually, as Seth Godin says in the quote that opens this Prologue, "Fix the mine."

It is not about patching up, reviving, and sending back on their way the many miserable employees who work for our organizations. It is about changing the organizations themselves and reclaiming our role in work being good whether we are CEO or at the front-line.

It makes me feel giddy inside that the data and the awareness that work isn't working is sitting squarely in the middle of research, workplace data, and thought leadership.

I do not see anyone arguing about whether we have a problem with work and that it is costing us.

But the real need at this point is to figure out what we can and must do about it.

Which is exactly what I offer with this book.

A roadmap, a prescription, and answers to two key questions. The first for business owners and leaders: "How can I make my organization both successful and good for people?" And the second for every one of us as an employee, "What is my role in making work good because I have, after all, achoice in working here?"

It can easily feel that it is business owners and leaders alone who must change and to blame them, labeling them as evil wrongdoers. If only it were that simple. I disagree wholeheartedly. We all have a role. We choose where to work. We agree to trade our good effort and output in exchange for a variety of currencies and because employers need us to contribute their great work to the work, we have infinite power as employees. We are not passive victims of the corporate machine. As author, speaker, and reality-based workplace expert Cy Wakeman says, "You are not a cog in a machine — far from it. You have more control than you think."

In my first book, *FIT Matters: How to Love Your Job,* my co-author and I focus explicitly on all the ways that employees can elevate their happiness at work.

With this book, *When Work is Good,* I call on people leaders, business owners, and employees to step-in and do their part.

Most importantly, take the actions I suggest. These steps can work if you are a family-held business with five employees or a large enterprise with offices around the globe.

But it only works if you work it.

Brave People Leaders who build work cultures in which people thrive all but guarantee themselves success in accomplishing mission, profit, value, and sustainability. And every single employee has a significant part in contributing to the collective thriving of any team they work with, daily.

After all, highly valued and accountable people build high-value and accountable organizations.

Let's make work good. The future depends on it.

Endnotes

1   https://www.hhs.gov/surgeongeneral/priorities/workplace-
    well-being/index.html
2   https://www.mckinsey.com/featured-insights/future-of-work/
    the-future-of-work-after-covid-19
3   https://www.gartner.com/en/insights/future-of-work

PART I
The Great Reframe

CHAPTER 1

Toxic is Bad!

*Leadership consistently emerged
as the top predictor of toxic culture.*

—Donald and Charles Sull,
MIT Sloan Management Review

A fellow workplace consultant and I were talking about how surprised we were that every industry and every company had miserable employees, no matter what the sector. Whether an organization is large or small, public or private, or whether the employees are white or blue collar, there's always a possibility that the conditions at work will be bad for some employees. This chapter builds on our definition of what counts in making a great workplace by expanding on the specific costs and impacts of toxicity at work.

I never cease to be amazed at the conditions in which we human beings can work. Some jobs are truly deplorable and toxic, from shipbreaking in the port town of Alang, India, to assembly-line work or coal mining in the United States. But work is unavoidable for most of us, so we humans do what we must.

For many of you reading this book, the odds are that although some of the jobs in your company might be dirty or difficult, they're likely more desirable than the worst jobs out there. But toxic work doesn't have to be deadly to cause harm.

And this is not NEW news. On the contrary, over the past 50 years, people *have* spoken up about terrible behavior at work, but they've been ignored and harmed further. And although whistleblower laws are designed to protect people, speaking truth to power is dangerous to whistleblowers in minor and catastrophic ways. As the Sull's report in their 2022 MIT Sloan article, "How to Fix a Toxic Culture," "More than a century of research has pinpointed a handful of elements of work design, such as overall workload and conflicting job demands, that consistently predict important outcomes, including toxic behavior."

We have all adjusted our expectations of work in ways that result in us not noticing what is bad for us. It's not uncommon for me to start working with a company and, during assessment, discover that the issues at hand have been going on for a long time. From long-overdue pay raises to tyrant leaders who aren't held accountable for bad behavior, organizations frequently protect and defend their status quo, even when, over time, it makes them inhospitable for humans.

Most of us know the frog in boiling water parable, where the frog placed in scalding water immediately fights to jump out because of the pain. But the frog placed in cool water that heats up slowly gets scalded as it incrementally adjusts to the conditions over time. At work, we're a bit like frogs.

Or at least we were until an invisible microbe caused the world to shut down and many workplaces to send people home. Many of us thought the shutdown would last weeks or months at the most, by we dragged through 2020 and well into 2021 with closed schools, canceled events, shelter in place, and workplaces in ways we had never seen before.

But as the pandemic was starting to ease (we thought) 48 million people left their jobs voluntarily in 2021, during the Great Resignation, and 4.3 million left in January 2022 in a trend that persists. Divergent theories were rampant about why people were quitting. One such theory was that young/entry-level workers didn't want to work hard anymore, especially when they could get paid to stay home due to federally funded job relief. This "they are just lazy" theory persisted, along with others such as the myth that compensation was the largest influencing factor, especially in low-wage jobs.

These theories were wrong, as Donald Sull, Charles Sull, and Ben Zweig[4] reported in their MIT Sloan Review Study. Their vast data set examined 14 million Glassdoor reviews and other data from employees who left their organization for any reason in their study period of April-September 2021. The data revealed the five top factors affecting why people quit their jobs:

- Toxic Corporate Culture
- Job Insecurity and Reorganization
- High Levels of Innovation
- Failure to Recognize Performance
- Poor Response to COVID-19

Of these, Toxic Corporate Culture was the single biggest predictor of turnover during the first six months of the Great Resignation, 10 times more powerful than compensation in predicting attrition. Now this is not new. Before COVID-19, employee turnover triggered by toxic culture was estimated to cost U.S. employers nearly $50 billion annually.

Breaking down the elements of a toxic culture, the Sull study revealed five attributes:

1. Disrespectful, defined as lack of consideration, courtesy, and dignity for others. This element rates as the one that matters most, and other words used included "dumpster fire," "dystopian," and "soul-sucking."
2. Non-inclusive, defined as inequity in key areas (i.e., racial, gender, LGBTQ, age, disability, cronyism, nepotism, and general inequity), leaving people feeling mistreated, not made to feel welcome, and not included in key decisions.
3. Unethical, defined as behavior that is dishonest or unethical and/or lack of compliance and common words used to describe related behaviors by employees were "unethical," "shady," "misleading," "false promises," "sugar-coating," and more.
4. Cutthroat, defined as backstabbing behavior and ruthless competition, often with associated words like "undermining," "dog-eat-dog," "thrown under the bus," and more.
5. Abusive, defined as sustained hostile behavior towards employees by managers, including bullying, harassment, and hostility

The Sull study proved what I have long seen in the organizations that I have worked with and heard from thousands of employee conversations over 30 years.

All five factors of the Sull study match what I see as the top contributors to Toxic Culture.

1. Lack of Inclusion.
The demographics of our work worlds are changing fast. The workforce is aging and will continue to do so; it's also becoming more diverse and, overall, more educated. Most people consider it a competitive advantage to have diverse minds working to solve problems; in other words, diversity is a good thing. Despite this, inclusion still stymies us at work. Women, people of color, LGBTQIA+, people with disabilities, and other marginalized groups continue to lag behind white men in their wages, power, and authority in almost every sector, despite the increase in their representation in the workplace.

In addition, the state of white men as a group is precarious. White men exhibit high rates of suicide, addiction, and alienation, in addition to being the majority of perpetrators of mass gun violence. We need a new way to talk about inclusion that leads to practicing inclusion, a way that honors and benefits everyone. White men, who are typically outside of diversity and inclusion conversations, must be invited in to learn, contribute, and benefit from exploring of how limiting systemic advantages to one group has created inequities at work that we can (and must) change.

Bravespace workplaces are ones in which race, gender, sexual orientation, and all the other things that make us both different and the same are discussed. Leaders of these workplaces eschew political correctness by tackling the truly hard issues that continue to stratify our society at home and at work.

Since the 2020 murder of George Floyd and the resultant public awareness of the deep racial divides that permeate every system in the USA, many organizations made public commitments to change, including increasing DEI Training, changing DEI hiring practices, offering more diverse cultural celebrations, establishing DEI Committees, hiring DEI focused staff and leaders, and modeling increased accountability.

Sadly, in late 2022 and early 2023, trends turned downward as layoffs disproportionately impacted HR and DEI roles. In the three months after protests globally arose from police violence, DEI job postings jumped 123%, according to data from the job site Indeed. Every organization in the land was finally serious about having a conscious and proactive approach to equity and inclusion at work. A Black colleague told me, "I have never been so popular with my white colleague at work as I am now. I hope their interest lasts." It appears as if it hasn't.

In 2023, listings for DEI roles dropped 19%, making DEI roles a most vulnerable function, with reported big hits from layoffs at Nike, Dell, Twitter, Amazon, and so many more.

What many underrepresented communities feared after George Floyd's death has largely manifested. System leaders and boards said they cared and were committed to meaningful, permanent change.

Apparently, their commitment only lasted as long as the optics looked good. Diversity, inclusion, equity, and belonging in every system are persistently threatened by political, binary extremism, fake news, and limp to non-existent long-term commitment to change.

I know that some organizations have remained "in" for the hard work of real belonging and equity, so please know that I see you out there staying the course. Good job!

2. Leaders Who are Bad for People/Feeling Disrespected/ Abusive Manager.

I have seen company after company ignore the dead weight of terrible managers for a host of reasons. The most common reason is that they are high producers and therefore, in a protected class, untouchable. When companies ignore bad managers, everyone suffers. The people who work for these toxic leaders wonder why no one is doing anything, they're demoralized, and they're confused by the gap between the values espoused by these leaders and the toxic world that the employees live in every day. With no attention from senior leaders, these situations usually get worse and result in employee churn, low team motivation and morale, and bad behaviors from team members. When the leader misbehaves, it signals that the behavior is okay and that no one minds. And inappropriate and bad behavior invites more of the same. There has been an uptick in bullying at work and in school since President Trump was elected, and that illustrates this dynamic: "If he can get away with it then I can too."

"It violates all the norms and the niceties of how one should behave," said Gary Namie, director and co-founder of the Workplace Bullying Institute. "What it's exposing is the very, very dark side of our society."

Leaders in Bravespace workplaces who are people-centered (they believe that people are what make companies great) and have demonstrated the ability to connect well with employees and colleagues are purposely invested in. And when leaders don't act in accordance with the cultural values and norms professed by the organization, there are swift consequences. Employees tune into, imprint, and copy what they see done by the leaders in their organization. In Bravespace workplaces, leaders who are bad for people are swiftly and effectively held accountable.

3.   Failure to Tell the Truth/Unethical Behavior.

When I work with companies of all types, a central piece of the work is the development of the norms and skills needed to have hard conversations. We often struggle mightily at work to tell our truth, to reveal what we feel, particularly when it comes to telling people about the impact they have on us, and to navigate conflicts. People at work have adopted behaviors that work around straight talk, including triangulation (telling our feelings to someone else, not the person we have an issue with), gossip (talking smack about someone behind their back), and avoidance (just not dealing with the situation), which is the most common behavior. This lack of truthfulness, and the masking of real feelings and needs, results in disconnection, isolation, and frustration at work. Decades of business ethics that kept emotions out of the workplace have resulted in those emotions leaking out unproductively, at inappropriate times, and in devastating ways, leading to stress-related illness and employee absenteeism.

The values and methods needed for handling conversations about difficult issues are commonplace in Bravespace workplaces. Leaders at every level are taught to be kind and clear while delivering direct feedback. Emotions at work are viewed as necessary for important (if hard) conversations that lead to creativity and innovations.

Toxic workplaces can look healthy on the outside, with a beautiful annual report, a fitness center, and ergonomic chairs. But what makes an organization fit for human life is the opposite of the three trends we just examined. These organizations stay healthy by drawing boundaries around work time and not expecting 24/7 digital connection, creating cultures of inclusion, designing time to think, fostering leaders who are good for people, and expecting (and modeling) real and true (even when difficult) conversations.

In addition to what the Sull Study revealed about why workers leave organizations, there is myriad evidence that there are other things that create toxicity at work, many of which COVID has brought into high relief. Here are the three big:

1. 24/7 Access and Our Device.

We are addicted to our devices. We carry them on our bodies and access them every few minutes. Our obsession with being always on means that our work is always ready to find us, activate us, and urge us to respond. A lot about this is good: it enables us to work anywhere, anytime. It speeds things up, so we can solve problems faster. It connects us globally. But the toxicity creeps in to violate and sabotage us. We need work to meet our basic needs, and our devices convince us that if we aren't always on, we're not good enough and we'll be regarded as not working as much as others. Speeding up response and thinking time also simultaneously erodes the quality of our decisions and our collaborative abilities. We work to contribute, to be seen, and to connect, and our devices seduce us into thinking that we should be connected all the time.

Digital media, email, text, and even collaboration hubs such as Slack are accessed by our devices, and they offer us things that are markedly different from our essential human need for connection. They're not necessarily bad—in fact, these applications often help us to be productive and connected—but the speed of our connection moves us fleetingly from one thing to another, with very little time to think and to add value by learning and growing. We need to feel supported at work, yet our fragmented interactions on these devices result in us often feeling more alone than ever. And we need to be able to make our lives work, but our devices have inserted themselves into every facet of our personal lives, showing up at our workouts, our dinner tables, our bedtimes with our kids, and even our bedrooms.

In addition, the media and advertising tell us that perfection is the ideal, which makes us feel that we're never good enough. And our devices make us feel even worse. We compare ourselves to our bosses' seeming heroism at working all hours and find ourselves wanting. We see other peoples' curated social media life and feel small because something is missing. We become numb and isolated, and the cycle continues.

Bravespace workplaces of the future define our device's role in our lives and the extent to which work intrudes on our personal lives.

A Bravespace workplace is one where we can show up as we are, both worthy and flawed, and do great things together, as human beings, with our strengths and weaknesses shaping how we partner and how we attack difficult tasks. As tools for productivity, our devices can be helpful, but when the devices themselves eat away our time and our confidence, we need to find an alternative. The rise of screen addiction among our children is a symptom of this toxic element of our workplaces that deadens our humanity; they learn from and copy us.

2.   Erosion of Time to Think.

Sean was a client who walked through my door seeking help. Promoted several times because of his hard work and keen mind, he was promoted again to manage a larger team. After six months on the job, he was flailing and losing the respect of his staff. Leaders like Sean often get promoted without understanding what work they'll have to let go of to assume their new role or without support from others in gaining that understanding. Instead of empowering and teaching his employees to use their creativity, discretion, and judgment to solve problems so that he wouldn't have to anymore, Sean was "heroically" doing it all. As a result, he lacked time in his meeting-filled days to bring forward that which was most precious to his employer.

Chris Carmichael, trainer of cycling phenom Lance Armstrong, revolutionized endurance training by incorporating rest into the rotation. Athletes can't go full tilt day after day and get better and better—their bodies need time to rebuild and recover. That applies to all of us. Our brains at work also need time to rest, recover, and think. Modern workplaces, with their frenetic pace, leave little time for simply thinking. The impact is that we don't do our best work. Time to think doesn't have to mean a month at an ashram in India. It can be a blank hour in the calendar, a walking reflection, or a conversation about ideas before action. Bravespace workplaces enable us to resist the urge to overdo. Time is overtly put aside for the people who work there to consider things, respond, analyze, and think. When that happens, the quality of ideas improves, people contribute more, and optimum results increase.

3. Lack of Flexibility and Work's Encroachment on our Lives.

Flexibility is the most often cited currency that workers desire today. For most of my adult life, it has felt as though flexibility was primarily sought by working mothers who were disproportionally burdened by the invisible workload of caring for children and elders and needed part-time options and some flexibility to tend to their families. But thankfully, it is not only women who desire the ability to flex their time at work, where they work, and how they work. Everyone is looking for options today that reduce commute time and increase quality of life.

Young people are more discerning about the quality of life they are seeking today. My employees in our small but mighty firm are open and transparent about the things that make their lives work. Needs such as caring for a young child, training a new puppy, therapy, workouts, and more stand out as requirements their employer needs to consider for real thriving. The days when employees are willing to sacrifice the quality of their life on the altar of "a good job" are, hopefully, behind us.

Even in careers that historically have been bastions requiring workaholic behavior, like medicine, things are starting to shift as young doctors refuse to take calls all the time or never make it home for dinner. The reality of most families being dual income and the awareness that personal thriving matters more than climbing the ladder is turning the tide on work taking an overblown role in the quality of our lives.

At the same time, workplaces continue to ask for heroism in every role and are slow to adapt to the flexibility needs of workers to make their lives work. Some big-name companies are forcing workers back to the office full-time while many are offering flexible or hybrid options.

Predictably, the flexibility for workers remains highest for employees with college degrees and in higher-wage jobs, reflecting the persistent inequity gap from the economic bottom to the top.

So, who are the ones building these toxic workplaces?

Consistently, we demonize toxic workplaces by imagining them to be "over there." If we are a small organization, we make up that mega-corporations are the ones running these evil empires. If we work in big tech, we may assume that small organizations are more damaging to workers.

I try hard to believe that People Leaders in workplaces everywhere are doing their best. Everyone I talk to (clients, program attendees, prospects) tells me they're trying hard to do their best, and I believe them.

But this leaves a paradox: if everyone is doing their best, who is creating toxic cultures and wreaking havoc on worker engagement? It must be some evil, tyrannical overlord, right?

I would prefer to demonize "bad leaders" elsewhere who are causing demoralized workforces.

But here's the rub: while the easy narrative is that unhealthy workplaces are about bad leaders, the truth is they are about you—and me too.

Even I after all these years consulting organizations and building resilient cultures, I do things that create unhealthy dynamics in my company that could be toxic for the people who work here.

Take these examples:

- In my stress, I dive in and micromanage someone because I am anxious, leaving them feeling disempowered and unseen.
- I overwork, sending the message that others should overwork too.
- My unconscious bias shows up, and I say something that causes someone to feel unseen or unsafe.

These examples may seem small, but they can add up.

I work hard to notice and name the ways I lead that inadvertently cause "toxicity" so that I can nip them in the bud with my team.

There's no magic formula for "good" or "bad" cultures.

Rather, through the small accumulation of tiny repairs, learnings, and decisions that we build robust, resilient cultures where people and organizations both thrive.

So, let's stop demonizing all of "them out there" who are causing harm by being bad leaders and instead spend our energy turning the lens inward to be the absolute best version of ourselves we can be for our organization and our employees.

We have the chance, amidst the potent and shocking realities of 2023 and beyond in the world of work to pay attention to what we know and make lasting change in how we work. But make work good is neither easy nor a one-step act. Let's look more deeply at what it means when work is good.

Endnotes

4 https://sloanreview.mit.edu/article/toxic-culture-is-driving-the-great-resignation/#article-authors

CHAPTER 2

The Messy Details of Defining *Good*

To define is to limit.

—Oscar Wilde, *The Picture of Dorian Gray*

On some days, I've loved going to work. Like the day I got to commute on my bike through the Italian countryside, where I worked with a terrific family-held business to strengthen their team. Or when I worked as a clinical counselor, and a patient was making a breakthrough, knew it, and shared her appreciation for my work, saying it made a difference. Or the hot summer days in my teens when, in a local ice cream shop, I made summertime feel festive for our entire community. I even loved the time my boss and I spent all night in a Kinko's, me with my breastfeeding baby in tow, refining our materials for a client gig the following day.

While I'm fortunate to have had these work experiences, not every day has been unicorns and rainbows. Some of my work experiences have been quite unpleasant—a few boring, some even hopeless, where I felt unseen, unimportant, or defeated. But throughout my career, I've often known that my work was making a difference, that what I did was good for someone, and that I was part of a team doing the thing what needed to be done. I know that, because of these experiences, I'm one of the lucky ones.

The thousands of people I've met as a consultant have shown me how lucky I've been. Sadly, I've heard story after story of folks who've struggled with boredom, isolation, stress, intimidation, fear, and frustration at work. That's why my work now consists of helping organizations find the right mix of actions and strategies that will activate the talents of their people so that they can achieve success.

I'm constantly thinking about how and why employees thrive and what makes a leader worth following. I notice the cacophony of voices in this field. I notice the thousands of business books published monthly. I notice the over 1.5 million consultants registered with the Bureau of Labor Statistics in the United States as of 2019[5] , and not just because I compete with them.

The business magazines and publications that cloud our airplane reading, mailboxes, and digital spheres—*Bloomberg*, *Fast Company*, *Inc.*, *Fortune*, etc.—often focus on one question: "What makes a company successful (aka great)?" For more than 150 years, our commerce system has answered this question with one word: *PROFIT*. Companies have historically focused on the increase in the gap between income and spending over time. As University of Chicago professor Jonathan Levy (2014)[6] says, while profit hasn't always meant the same thing, it always implies growth over time, often incessant growth. The economic models we've inherited are outdated. As British economist Kate Raworth (2017)[7] says, "The citizens of 2050 are being taught an economic mindset that is rooted in the textbooks of 1950, which in turn are based on the theories of 1850." Relentless focus on quarter-over-quarter, year-over-year growth has had dire consequences.

First and foremost, we now live on a planet deeply scarred by our use of natural resources, and climate change is rapidly affecting production, resources, and economies (Pachauri and Meyer 2014)[8]. Second, we're seeing a staggering accumulation and concentration of wealth by a few select shareholders, resulting in wage stagnation and a crippling wage gap (Bloomberg 2018)[9]. Third, employees are increasingly seeking purpose and meaning at work and are looking for ways to have a life and a lifestyle that works for them and their families (Gallup 2017b)[10]. Because of these changes, the conversations around how we work and what makes a company great are changing.

Employees ask themselves and their employers questions such as: "Does this job offer monetary compensation enough to cover the expenses of my lifestyle?" "Is there room for my personal development?" "Do my values and priorities match those of my workplace?" Companies listed in *Fortune* magazine's annual *100 Best Companies to Work For* and the *Great Place to Work* surveys boast benefits such as dedicated mindfulness rooms, healthy company culture, or "family" vibes. Their advertised assets point to the notion that employees today seek much more from work than the exchange of time for money.

Much of the media's attention on the modern workplace focuses on on large public companies, especially the mega-tech companies Apple, Facebook, Google, and Amazon. We often look to these as examples of how to organize people, what perks and benefits to offer employees, and what best practices for management and culture. Yet, despite the concentration of wealth in companies like these, small businesses—defined as having fewer than 500 employees—still represent 99.7% of employer firms in the United States (Small Business Administration 2012)[11].

Most of us work for small businesses, yet the conversations about great places to work focus on mega-corporate America. This means that the real variation in great workplaces goes unrecognized in popular media outlets. People are miserable in both large and small workplaces, but people often think about big companies when it comes to workplace health and culture because that's what we see in popular media.

But small organizations play a significant role in how we work, and they also have some advantages when it comes to being fit for human life. *Small Giants* by *Inc.* editor Bo Burlingham (2016)[12] highlights some of these advantages, including:

- The ability to change more quickly and more often
- The flexibility to customize solutions
- The ability (in private companies) to make investments and plan without having to report monthly profitability to Wall Street (protecting gross margins without compromising values)
- A strong focus on purpose as a driver
- Leadership deeply rooted in practical values
- Strong community connections and relationships
- Easier-to-cultivate meaningful relationships with customers, suppliers, employees, and stakeholders

In this book, I discuss practices in all-sized organizations, but I'll focus on concepts, ideas, and tools to help leaders in small to mid-sized companies transform their organizations into brave, people-centered workplaces to achieve the results they seek. Of course, the concepts, ideas, and tools I describe in *Bravespace Workplace* are certainly relevant to large or mega-corporations and will work there, still my emphasis is mostly on helping smaller organizations.

I spend my days asking people what elements make their work dreadful and what brings them personal fulfillment and engagement. The answers I get are unique and specific. As my co-author Cammie Dunaway and I wrote in *Fit Matters: How to Love Your* Job (Carrick and Dunaway 2017)[13], defining *great* is more about determining the right place *for you* is a general assessment of greatness. Work fit (distinctly different from "fitting in") isn't easy to come by, and it requires solutions that are unique for each person.

There are some general features that people everywhere need. We human beings want everything that makes up a good life: love, play, challenge, community, giving back, freedom, safety, celebration, comfort, and health. We need the ability to support ourselves, to contribute, and to believe that what we do makes a difference to someone. People define *great* in a whole host of different ways, many of them highly personal. "Can I flex my hours to meet my personal needs?" "Is my commute to work long?" "Do I like my co-workers?" "Do I think my employer is paying me fairly?" "Am I the only one of me (Black, gay, disabled, etc.)?"

In general, these questions aren't being asked often or early enough. According to the 2023 Gallup employee engagement data, only 32% of full-and part-time employees working for organizations now are engaged, while 18% are actively disengaged. Active disengagement increased[14] by two percentage points from 2021 and four points from 2020. I see in my own work that, unfortunately, many people give up their pursuit of a well-fitting job, persuaded by the belief that work is just a necessary evil, something you have to do to pay the bills. This apathy leads to misery, lost time, lost energy, and lost money.

We, humans, work a lot. And our culture of 24/7 digital connection, urgency, and immediacy means that, regardless of how many hours we formally work each week, people everywhere report that they're overwhelmed. For some, it's the grueling demands of a professional role that knows no boundaries in terms of when we're on or off. For others it's the relentlessness of working two or three or four different jobs to cobble together enough money to support a family, leaving precious little time for anything but work. Although the Bureau of Labor Statistics (2018)[15] says that the average American full-time worker over age 16 works 34.5 hours a week, most people, when you ask them, report that they think they work much more or "all the time." As journalist Brigid Schulte (2014)[16] says in her bestselling book, *Overwhelmed: Work, Love, and Play When No One Has the Time*, "Our perception of time is indeed our reality."

We spend more time at work than sleeping, eating, playing, or with family and friends (Smith Major et al. 2002)[17]. Life is too short for our work hours to be wasted in misery.

So, What Do We Really Need?

For most of us, a great many of our needs are met by our work-places, so happiness in life is strongly correlated to happiness in work. We crave being connected to others, contributing to something meaningful beyond self, and adding value to something that matters. When you feel good at work, you have energy and the capacity for creativity and partnership. This, in turn, creates a virtuous cycle in which the better you feel, the more you contribute at work. People are drawn to you in partnership, and you get things done well with others.

People are not machines. Since we're human, it's important to our very survival that we add value and find purpose at work. Psychologist Abraham Maslow (1943)[18] places meaningful work (as connected to self-esteem and self-actualization) in a critical spot in his hierarchy of needs for our human thriving, right behind physiological and safety needs. As author and professor Barry Schwartz (2015)[19] said in his book, *Why We Work*, "To be satisfied with our work, we typically need a belief in the purpose of what we do."

Abraham Maslow placed our human need for social connection behind physiological and safety needs, but current pundits have disagreed and argued that our need for human connection is as essential to us as food, water, shelter, safety, and security. As Simon Sinek said in *Leaders Eat Last*, "Our need to feel a sense of belonging or connection with others is not just a feeling we get; it is a survival mechanism." Connecting with people is a survival mechanism, and one of our primary places for connection is at work.

One of the more influential studies about the relevance of human connection at work is the January 2023 Surgeon General's Report on "Workplace Well-Being and Mental Health," published by Dr. Vivek Murthy, which highlights the pressing need to address the mental health of employees. The report illustrates how the COVID-19 pandemic brought the relationship between work and well-being into more precise focus for many U.S. workers. According to recent surveys:

- 76% of U.S. workers in a 2021 survey reported at least one symptom of a mental health condition[20] (anxiety, depression), an increase of 17 percentage points in just two years.
- 81% of workers reported that they will be looking for workplaces that support mental health[21] in the future.
- 84% of respondents reported at least one workplace factor that had a negative impact on their mental health[22].

The report argues that mental illness can have debilitating effects on individuals' productivity, job satisfaction, and work relationships. It highlights that employers who fail to address mental health concerns in the workplace will cause negative consequences for the individual employee, the organization, and for society as a whole.

Coming on the heels of the Global Pandemic, the world at large is ready to listen. The Surgeon General offers a framework of five conditions everyone need from work.

Conditions We Need from Work, U.S. Surgeon General's Office 2023

- **Protection from Harm**: Creating the conditions for physical and psychological safety is a critical foundation for ensuring mental health and well-being in the workplace. To promote practices that better assure protection from harm, workplaces can:
  o Prioritize workplace physical and psychological safety
  o Enable adequate rest
  o Normalize and support focusing on mental health
  o Operationalize Diversity, Equity, Inclusion, and Accessibility (DEIA) norms, policies, and programs

- **Connection and Community**: Fostering positive social interaction and relationships in the workplace supports worker well-being. To promote practices that better assure connection and community, workplaces can:
  o Create cultures of inclusion and belonging
  o Cultivate trusted relationships
  o Foster collaboration and teamwork

- **Work-Life Harmony**: Professional and personal roles can create work and non-work conflicts. To promote practices that better assure work-life harmony, workplaces can:
  o Provide more autonomy over how work is done
  o Make schedules as flexible and predictable as possible
  o Increase access to paid leave
  o Respect boundaries between work and non-work time

- **Mattering at Work**: People want to know that they matter to those around them and that their work matters. Knowing you matter has been shown to lower stress, while feeling like you do not can increase the risk for depression. To better assure a culture of mattering at work, workplaces can:
  - Provide a living wage
  - Engage workers in workplace decisions
  - Build a culture of gratitude and recognition
  - Connect individual work with organizational mission

- **Opportunities for Growth**: When organizations create more opportunities for workers to accomplish goals based on their skills and growth, workers become more optimistic about their abilities and more enthusiastic about contributing to the organization. To promote practices that better assure opportunities for growth, workplaces can:
  - Offer quality training, education, and mentoring
  - Foster clear, equitable pathways for career advancement
  - Ensure relevant, reciprocal feedback

It's gratifying to me that the things I've known through my research and experience are validated by one of North America's highest health authorities. I think everyone—but business leaders in particular—stand to gain from understanding this new report.

"Work is an important social determinant of health."—U.S. Surgeon General's Report "Workplace Well-being and Mental Health"

If you are not working in healthcare, you may be unfamiliar with what a "social determinant of health" is. A social determinant of health is anything non-medical that nonetheless influences health outcomes.

So, people's daily life conditions influence their health. To say that work is a social determinant of health is to say "work impacts our health."

It's not enough to stop at this realization because it doesn't indicate anything about good or ill health. As an experiment, let's imagine two organizations, one where the leaders optimize for output above health and another where leaders optimize for health above all else.

When optimizing for output above everything leaders would make decisions about profit, strategy, and outcome without regard for human lives. It's easy to picture the extreme: forced-labor camps where death, misery, and sickness are the costs paid for high achievement.

If you care about people, you've probably wondered, "How can I optimize for output without causing ill health?" But let's jump to the other organization, where positive health is critical.

In this extreme, it's easy to picture an unaccomplished utopia where people drift from pleasure to pleasure without getting anything done.

Now you're wondering, "How can I optimize for human thriving without sacrificing the very needs of the business?"

I've seen countless leaders get stuck in this false dichotomy. The reality is that human thriving impacts organizational success for the better. Here's how I guide my clients through this sticky misconception. As you read each statement, check if you agree with each one.

1. We spend more time at work than anywhere else, assuming full-time work.
2. Because we spend so much time at work, it's a vital part of our lives that shapes our overall health and well-being.
3. When we thrive at work, we function better in the world (by feeling a sense of contribution and purpose and making money to meet our needs and to cool stuff) and cost society less (in terms of the costs we share—impacts of poverty, emergency services, social services, unemployment, and more).
4. When we thrive at work, our companies save money and resources (in costs of absenteeism, workplace injury, litigation, turnover, low motivation and morale, poor service and quality, and more.)
5. When we thrive at work, our companies create more value and achieve better results (through the aggregated output of an engaged, healthy, long-lived workforce).
6. When our companies thrive, workers also benefit from increased wages, opportunities, and benefits, and our communities thrive from our philanthropy and continued community investment (buying goods, etc).

This process we've just explored is what I call the Virtuous Cycle of Work. I often summarize this cycle by saying that People Make Organizations Great.

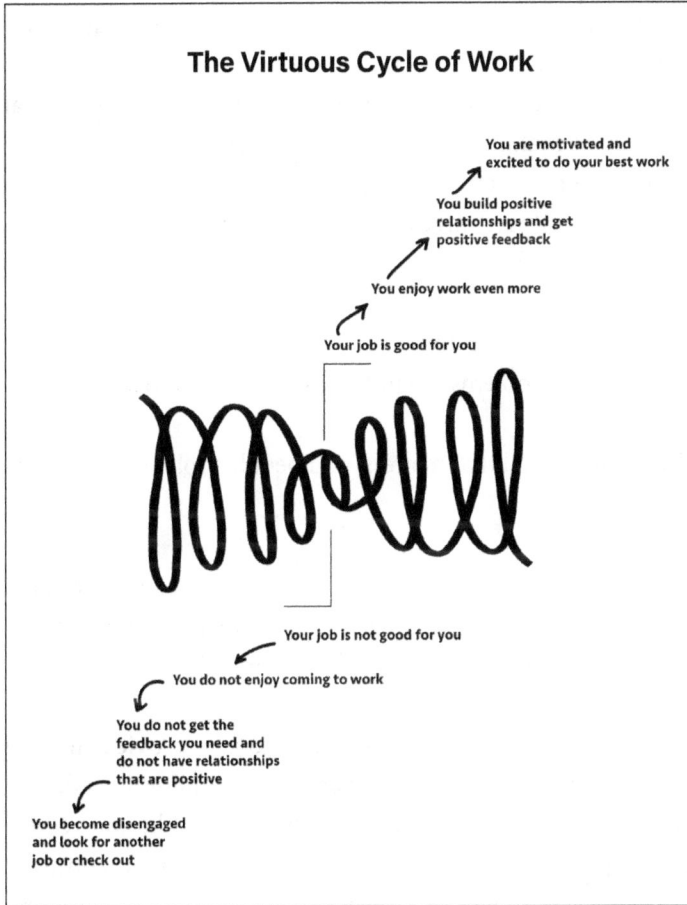

The Virtuous Cycle of Work

You are motivated and excited to do your best work

You build positive relationships and get positive feedback

You enjoy work even more

Your job is good for you

Your job is not good for you

You do not enjoy coming to work

You do not get the feedback you need and do not have relationships that are positive

You become disengaged and look for another job or check out

But justifying an investment of company resources into human thriving continues to be a hard sell, which is why human suffering persists in modern workplaces.

I've struggled to convince leaders to invest in human thriving. Throughout my career, I've had to prove the ROI of their investments, even for leaders who see the moral and ethical urgency of making workplaces fit for human life. Now, these leaders are not stupid. So why is it so hard to find leaders who invest adequate resources in human thriving? It has to do with the internalized stories about *why we work*, such as:

> "Profit is the North Star."
> "People problems are mysterious and hard to solve."

But profit isn't all that matters, and people problems aren't unsolvable.

We're long overdue for new ways of working. As they say in Dr. Murthy's report, there's no better time to make your workplace an "engine of mental health and well-being."

The report recommends that employers provide mental health resources and support for their employees, educate employees on the importance of mental health, and reduce the stigma associated with mental illness. Implementing of such recommendations can improve the overall well-being of workers and create a more empathetic and inclusive work environment.

We bring our human need to connect with other people right smack dab into our jobs and workplaces. Countless times, when I'm asked to support a client for culture development, team health, or leadership effectiveness, I find that the central problem is that employees are feeling unseen, alone, and unsupported at work. As Patrick Lencioni (2002)[23], blockbuster author on teams and organizations, says, "More than anything else at work, people crave being seen, valued, and feeling like they contribute to work that matters (in any role at any level)."

Based on my experience with hundreds of organizations, thousands of individuals, and countless examples of both workplace misery and workplace thriving, combined with the excellent research of others about organizational effectiveness and leadership impact, I have developed a short list of the needs that work should fulfill for us as human beings. These seven needs, developed before the Surgeon General's Report "Workplace Well-Being and Mental Health," fit perfectly in their model. Fulfilling these seven needs will facilitate the extent to which every one of us can bring our best ideas, our fullest energy, and our hardest effort to our work (drum roll please):

Seven Needs that Work Should Fulfill

1. To meet our basic requirements – to make enough money or non-cash compensation to provide food, clothing, shelter, and safety.
2. To contribute – to do something that matters to someone.
3. To be seen – and known.
4. To connect – in authentic ways, with other people.

5. To learn – and become better.
6. To feel supported – to be able to be brave.
7. To make our lives work – to be able to do the things that matter to us and are ours to do.

When we have these ingredients at work, we can bring our best to it in the fullest sense. And when we bring our full selves to work, we thrive, and our team and organization get results. My most cherished work memories are the moments when my gifts were perfectly suited to the problem and situation I faced *and* I was able to bring my full self to it. In those moments, I felt brave, even when I was extremely frightened, I could do the hard thing.

What makes work good? Being fit for the human beings who make it good and being designed purposefully to be so. Great organizations are employers that consciously and proactively invest time, energy, and resources to make work good. I define these organizations as Bravespace workplaces, where people can show up as they are, both worthy and flawed, and do great things together. Bravespace workplaces activate, enliven, and tenderly support the complex humans we are so that we can bring our complete selves to work every day.

Endnotes

5   Bureau of Labor Statistics. 2018. "BLS Data Viewer." https://
    beta.bls.gov/dataViewer/view/timeseries/CES0500000002.

6   Levy, Jonathan. 2014. "Accounting for Profit and the History of
    Capital." *Critical Historical Studies* 1, No. 2 (Fall), 171–214.

7   Raworth, Kate. 2017. *Doughnut Economics.* New York: Random
    House Business.

8   Pachauri, R.K., and L.A. Meyer, eds. 2014. *Climate
    Change 2014: Synthesis Report.* Contribution of Working
    Groups I, II and III to the Fifth Assessment Report of the
    Intergovernmental Panel on Climate Change. Geneva,
    Switzerland: IPCC.

9   Bloomberg. 2018. "Where Have All the Public Companies
    Gone?" (April 9). https://www.bloomberg.com/view/
    articles/2018-04-09/ where-have-all-the-u-s-public-
    companies-gone.

10 Gallup. 2017b. *State of the Global Workplace.* https://www.
    gallup.com/ workplace/238079/state-global-workplace-2017.
    aspx.

11 Small Business Administration. 2012. "Frequently Asked
    Questions." SBA Office of Advocacy.

12 Burlingham, Bo. 2016. *Small Giants: Companies That Choose to
    Be Great Instead of Big.* New York: Portfolio.

13 Carrick, Moe, and Cammie Dunaway. 2017. *Fit Matters: How
    to Love Your Job.* Palmyra, VA: Maven House.

14 https://www.gallup.com/workplace/468233/employee-
    engagement-needs-rebound-2023.aspx

15 Bureau of Labor Statistics. 2018. "BLS Data Viewer." https://
    beta.bls.gov/dataViewer/view/timeseries/CES0500000002.

16 Schulte, Brigid. 2014. *Overwhelmed: Work, Love, and Play When No One Has the Time.* New York: Sarah Crichton Books.

17 Smith Major, Virginia, Katherine J. Klein, and Mark G. Ehrhart. 2002. "Work Time, Work Interference with Family, and Psychological Distress." *Journal of Applied Psychology* 87 (3): 427–36.

18 Maslow, Abraham H. 1943. "A Theory of Human Motivation," *Psychological Review* 50 (4): 370–96.

19 Schwartz, Barry. 2015. *Why We Work.* New York: Simon and Schuster, TED Books.

20 https://www.mindsharepartners.org/ mentalhealthatworkreport-2021

21 https://www.apa.org/pubs/reports/work-well-being/2022-mental-health-support#:~:text=A%20majority%20 (81%25)%20of,into%20their%20future%20job%20decisions.

22 https://hbr.org/2021/10/its-a-new-era-for-mental-health-at-work

23 Lencioni, Patrick. 2002. *The Five Dysfunctions of a Team.* San Francisco: Jossey-Bass.

CHAPTER 3

HR is Broken
and Tired

*"The great reset requires HR to examine our practices,
shed the ones that no longer serve our companies and
employees, and build anew ... It requires a shift away from
prescribed playbooks of HR programs and a willingness to
pilot and adopt new practices. It will be centered on employee[24]
experience and co-created[25] with our employees."*

—Lars Schmidt, Fast Company

One of my most popular free webinars in 2021 had the title
HR Can't Save You Now.

I offered it because most companies, frustrated, overwhelmed,
and not sure what to do regarding the upside-down people
dimensions of their business, were turning to HR for answers.

- How should we design hybrid work policies?
- How should we handle vaccine mandates?
- What will work for remote performance management?
- When and how can we get people back to work?

Leaders in every sector were hoped that Human Resources, an established function in their organizations often seen as administrative and disconnected from ROI, would have the answers to their enormous people problems.

HR leaders were rapidly overwhelmed. They faced tremendous pressure to heroically save organizations from collapse. When the whole world shut down, the duality that existed for HR as a business function was profound. On the one hand, HR saw an 87% increase in demand, according to Indeed. On the other, HR professionals today are burned out and overwhelmed as their roles have, of necessity, come out of the closets where they had essentially been sitting historically of compliance and administration. The paradox of being profoundly needed alongside leaders at every level combined with a lack of preparedness to navigate the new world of work, has created a terrible double bind for HR itself.

Let's take a ride in the way-back machine to look at the roots of HR, how it lost its way, and what the future holds.

Human Resources has its roots in the late 1800s and early 1900s, during the Industrial Revolution in the United States. The rise of large-scale manufacturing and increasing demands on labor drove companies to recognize the importance of managing their workforce more systematically. One of the earliest known to be practicing HR as we know it today was the National Cash Register Company in Dayton, Ohio, where employee records were kept and a personnel department was established.

In the early 1900s, HR began to evolve more formally, with pioneering works such as Frederick Taylor's "Scientific Management" theory that emphasized efficiency and productivity. In 1913, the US government enacted the Department of Labor, which included the Bureau of Labor Statistics and the newly created Employment Service. The Employment Service offered employment information and created a pool of job candidates for employers.

During World War II, the demand for labor dramatically increased, creating a need for more organized HR functions, such as recruitment and training. The HR field continued to evolve, with notable milestones, such as the Civil Rights Act of 1964, which outlawed discrimination in the workplace and championed equal pay.

Over time, the role of HR has grown to include administrative and legal compliance, compensation and benefits, workforce safety and equity, diversity and inclusion, training and development, and more.

Despite the historical expansion of human resources, in many instances the function has evolved to serve as one that benefits the company itself by driving efficiency and performance without costly employee relations issues. Despite what many employees imagine, human resources is not specifically about the care and feeding of the organization's most precious resource: its people.

The result? HR continues to be overburdened with responsibilities that it should not carry alone and is often asked to miraculously solve. Today, HR is held accountable for many areas that operational leaders ought to own while being bloated with inefficiencies and administrative work that will not facilitate transformation towards the Bravespace workplaces of tomorrow. A few examples:

1. Traditional hiring models are slow, expensive, and not very effective, resulting in a lack of transparency and bias for hiring and screening.

2. Despite some progress, HR departments themselves, and the field as a whole, struggle with unconscious bias and inequality as it impacts hiring, salary negotiation, and performance feedback.

3. Claims of discrimination and harassment are often handled inconsistently or obscurely. While employees think of HR as the function that will take care of them, the function itself is often tasked with prioritizing risk mitigation and protecting the organizations assets.

4. HR has not upskilled its own practice to keep pace with furiously fast changes in workforce demographics including the currency of flexibility, work from anywhere realities, AI and technology disrupters, the changing needs of People Leaders, the challenges to culture with remote work, diversity, equity, inclusion, and belonging as critical issues for retention and market share, employee mental health and well-being, and more.

5. Lack of strategic leadership: In some cases, HR departments are not effectively integrated into an organization's overall strategy and vision, leaving them vulnerable to layoffs and

lack of operational authority (an estimated 28% of the tech layoffs of 2022/2023 were in HR).

6. Resistance to change: HR as a function can be resistant to innovative or disruptive changes, such as technology adoption, agile structures, and flexible work arrangements. This rigidity might hamper the traditional HR role's ability to remain relevant and effective in managing the organization's workforce.

7. HR is often ineffectual in meaningfully creating conditions for employee thriving and instead is relegated to protecting the entity from litigation. Confusion about the role of HR contributes to low trust and confidence of employees as to whether HR is invested in them as humans who work there. Policies and rules, while well-intended, need to be equally met with rigorous and candid conversations at all levels to reinforce the values of the company and the desired behaviors.

What is the future of HR?

It is time for a radical new view of the role of tending to human beings to make work good.

And the central effort happens by leaders at every level, driven by an accountable business owner or C-Suite, not solely by HR. HR of tomorrow will likely have a role, particularly in organizations of over 100 employees who need systems support and operational support to build efficient ways to leverage the talents of people, navigate hiring and exits, and ensure compliance, benefits, and compensation are clear and appropriate.

But since people in organizations know their workplace primarily through their relationship with their leader, this is where organizations committed to unbreakable cultures will focus.

A few specific ideas for how the people side of every organization might be managed tomorrow in ways that leverage HR and put people and culture in the hands of every leader include:

1. The executive dashboard or KPI list includes responsibility for the well-being of people, the development of leaders who are good for people, and the stewardship of culture in addition to mission, product, and revenue goals and measures.

2. Measures for making work good for people lie with the senior-most leaders, not HR. The Finance Department, for example, is not responsible for every single budget and financial management decision of every leader on station. Rather, Finance supports fiscal decision-making with solid processes and tools, which is what HR can do in the realm of people and culture.

3. HR departments become focused on the whole employee experience, working closely with People Leaders at every level to ensure that employees have equal access to internal resources and opportunities and know how to find the resources for their thriving at work.

4. Performance reviews will migrate away from annual rating and ranking systems to frequent two-way conversations between managers and their people to share feedback, learn together, and increase engagement and learning.

5. New options for well-being that include mental health and work-life integration support will be crafted and sourced

alongside other employee health initiatives (including flexible benefits).

6. Company culture will be a key strategic initiative and people or HR staff will support measurement and tracking of cultural health components.

7. Managing remote work will be a clear focus for most organizations with clear policies and expectations that are equitably applied.

8. Recruitment and promotion will become even more critically scrutinized to source diverse candidates for every role and ensure that they succeed once they join the organization and get promoted.

9. Companies will regularly report on their progress in DEIB to their customers, stakeholders, and employees.

10. Career pathing will include expert individual contributor roles in addition to managerial tracks.

11. HR will leverage technology to automate mundane people tasks and empower employees with autonomy for their own contracting, benefits, performance conversations, and more.

The future Bravespace workplaces that make work good will manifest new and effective alliances and partnerships with human resources, organizational development, and recruiting professionals and senior leaders as a business strategy that focuses on the essential truth that people are every organizations most important asset.

This essential mindset will mean that tending to people becomes good business, rather than a cost center, and rises in significance to the very top of every organization.

Human Resources as a professional practice area will need to take a long, hard look at what it has evolved into in recent decades and become a more strategic, brave, relevant, and provocative part of the organization than ever before. The name "human resources" goes away and evolves into a more aptly names center of organizational excellence, pulling from the behavioral science of organizational psychology and development into a new, merged superpower for every company.

Maybe tomorrows HR Leaders will have titles like Chief Community Officer, Chief Curator of People Experience, or Chief of People's Well-Being at Work.

Endnotes

24 https://www.mckinsey.com/capabilities/people-and-organizational-performance/our-insights/the-new-possible-how-hr-can-help-build-the-organization-of-the-future

25 https://hbr.org/2018/03/co-creating-the-employee-experience

PART II
Humans, Thriving

CHAPTER 4

The Sanctity of Work

Without ambition one starts nothing.
Without work one finishes nothing.
The prize will not be sent to you.
You have to win it.

—Ralph Waldo Emerson

Do you remember the first job you loved?

Mine meant the world to me.

I thought I was in trouble when my high school guidance counselor asked to see me. Had I done something bad? Did I need supervision?

Neither of these was true. He had a job available and thought I could do it well. So, I began working at **Four Seas Ice Cream**[26], in Centerville, Massachusetts. I was intimidated and scared— all of the cooler, older kids worked at the shop—but I said yes, primarily for the pay. I jumped in with both feet, despite my trepidation, and that job grew to mean much more to me than just a paycheck.

Through high school and college, I worked summers at Four Seas. We worked six days a week, sometimes doing split shifts, and the work was hard and dirty. I remember being sticky up to my armpits, stinking of sour cream, and literally running around to serve an endless line of summer customers. Even more importantly, though, I remember feeling the bond of being part of a team and the reward that comes from working hard.

I was needed. I felt competent. I felt trusted. I felt part of something bigger. I felt less dependent. I knew someone would notice if I missed a shift. My co-workers became my friends over time. I funded college and grad school mainly from my income. After seven years, I grieved when life changes required me to stop working there.

Those early days formed an impression on me that has never faded (and that I write about often): **we need the psychological as well as economic benefits we get from contributing to work.**

Real thriving at work, in any job, is about knowing we are contributing to something bigger than ourselves.

Work is part of identity and central to our sense of ourselves. Even at age 16, when I first donned my uniform at Four Seas Ice Cream, I felt the powerful benefit of contributing to something that mattered. Yes, it was only ice cream. But to the scores of people who crowded the shop from Memorial Day to Labor Day, it was pure pleasure, a joyful treat, a hallmark of summer, and a break from the routine. And I, the server, saw the smiles on people's faces that gave my job a greater purpose than my paycheck.

What Work Does for Us

I recently sent buckets of old family photos to get digitized.

Going through them, I found a picture of my mom, my siblings, and me getting off a plane in 1964.

There I am, the blonde in the red dress shading my eyes from the sun.

And that's my mom, holding my brother on her hip.

When this was taken, my mom was living an American Dream: she'd dropped out of Stanford University to home make, looking after me and my siblings while her young husband, my dad, made the dough as an architect. The plane trip was when we moved to Boston for him to attend Harvard School of Design—a big move.

Like any dreamscape, the more I look back on this time, the more I see its weirdness and fragmentations.

My parent's marriage was falling apart. My dad struggled with alcoholism and mental health. And as much as he tried to fulfill his role as Bread Winner, he was always better at playing Starving Artist.

Not long after this photo, my mom found herself single, without formal education, career path, or means of supporting herself.

(Note of credit to my dad: he tended to his health and stayed sober until his death. I have many fond and meaningful memories with him.)

This moment of my childhood in the photo captured my family's transformation that formed many of my fundamental insights about the world of work.

I watched my mom return to school while working nights as a nurse. Over the years, she rose into a nursing leadership position where she navigated a robust and fulfilling 35-year career.

I imagine she felt terrified to have the life she'd expected—a husband who'd provide, while she stayed home—taken from her. I imagine how angry she must have been at her powerlessness to fix things and her frustration at being left without the money she needed to buy us food and clothing.

Yet, as she worked, she found power. She was among many women who picked up the frayed threads of the nuclear family model and found a viable path forward.

She told me over and over again how important it was that I had money, credit, and a way to support myself.

During that time, she told me and showed me **the Sanctity of Work—how devoting oneself to showing up, contributing, and earning money can be a form of salvation, a means to a fulfilled life.**

I think it was my mom's way of expressing herself as a liberated woman.

By the time she was able to retire, part of me expected she'd be eager to shake off the burden of her work.

So, I was surprised when her first move was to take a six-month job as the Head Gardener at a remote Wyoming Guest Ranch.

By the time she died, I knew her job was one of the highlights of her life—she relished that period. My mom went to work for the cash and its corollaries. But she stayed for the Sanctity of Work—the way it gave her a place to be, a purpose to fulfill, community, and learning.

While the world she left—a world where women aren't recognized for the full scope of their contributions and fragile masculinity works like a poison—still has vestiges today, my mom shines brightly to me as a stalwart pioneer demonstrating how central work is to our identities.

She supported me through every twist of my career, even when the work, travel, and stress threatened to overwhelm me, and my family, too, suffered divorce and hardship.

When I turned 50, she asked me what I was looking forward to in my sixth decade.

From a tired, weary place, I said something snarky, like, "I want to rest!"

She replied, "Oh, no, keep working. Your 50s are when everything finally comes together."

Somewhere along the way, my mom learned how precious work is.

Even in her last days, across many years of retirement, she proudly told people she was a nurse.

Every time she did, her eyes sparkled.

Being a nurse gave her power. It gave her knowledge. It was something she'd achieved and was immensely proud of.

I've returned to the Sanctity of Work throughout my life when the going gets tough. And I've found my mom's wisdom to ring true, even all these decades later.

Here are a few more words on the Sanctity of Work:

- The Sanctity of Work doesn't mean work is the most important thing in your life.
- It doesn't mean you must submit to unreasonable levels of stress and exhaustion or sacrifice what you care about to serve some machine.
- It doesn't over-index on productivity over well-being or production over loving the people in your life.
- Rather, **it's a generous mindset that encompasses the varied and very real, very human, and straightforward needs we have from work and work's unique capacity to fill them.**

Needs like:

- Our need to have somewhere to be, even when we don't want to get out of bed.
- Our need to build things with a community and connect with others.
- Our need to be seen for our unique ideas and contributions.
- Our need to make ends meet for ourselves and our families.
- Our need to practice doing hard things because it feels good.
- Our need for the tiresome hours of our lives to *mean* something.
- Our need to learn and grow right up to the end of our days.

The best employers are the ones who can recognize and embrace the Sanctity of Work.

Those employers are the ones who design their workplaces with the Sanctity of Work in mind.

They design their time-off policies with this sanctity in mind.

They structure their compensation packages and training plans with the Sanctity of Work in mind.

They reward leaders who are good for people with an eye to the primacy of the relationship we have with our boss to thriving.

They empower people to define and create their sacred work because it matters.

And it just so happens that when they do all of this, they get good employees and,—voila—the organization thrives, its value grows, the mission is met, and profitability happens.

Since Margaret (my mom) passed almost two years ago, she visits me in my dreams nightly. When I wake, I ache with longing for her presence, but I am enlivened by her voice in my head, encouraging me to go to work.

Endnote

26 https://www.fourseasicecream.com/

CHAPTER 5

Workplace = Bravespace
A New Definition

Brave doesn't always involve grand gestures.
Sometimes brave looks more like staying when you
want to leave, telling the truth when all you want to do
is change the subject.

—Shauna Niequist

There's a deepening anxiety that robots and technology will remove humans from the workplaces of tomorrow. But doing so would be a mistake because the profound differentiator for most companies remains the people who work for them. People at work who bring empathy, connection, magic, warmth, understanding, joy, creativity, imagination, beauty, and innovation to organizations as they build things, serve customers, and meet their mission.

To crack the code on making work good, I propose a new way to describe healthy, or great, workplaces: *Bravespace.* In Bravespace workplaces, the absolute best in the human beings who work there is cultivated, despite our imperfect and complicated human motivations, needs, and issues. In Bravespace workplaces, people can face the risks, emotional exposure, uncertainty, and vulnerability that come with work, knowing that their courage is supported and invited. The leaders of Bravespace workplaces know that people aren't machines, and treat them accordingly. People are strong and fragile, smart and thoughtless, complex and basic, diverse and similar. We are complicated and beautiful, and predicting what we'll do in different circumstances is almost impossible.

People cannot be defined in one paradigm or put in one box. Bravespace workplaces are people-centered because their leaders deeply understand that people make all the good things happen at work. In this chapter I'll explore the currencies that matter to people today at work, as well as expand on the implications of a new definition of work for how we run organizations tomorrow.

Happiness Isn't Enough

Throughout my career, I've heard leaders from all sectors, when interpreting my overarching messages to them, say, "So, we need to do things that make people happy at work, right?" They think happiness is a permanent state we can create with a magic wand. Creating workplaces fit for human life—and paying conscious attention to the soft stuff of people-centered leadership and culture—is not simply about making people happy at work.

What, after all, is "happy"? Happiness in Shakespearean times was equated to prosperity and good fortune. Going further back to ancient Greece (Aristotle 2011)[27], "Happiness . . . signifie[d] more than mere sentiment or feeling, more than the pleasure of the moment or even of a series of satisfied desires. [Happiness] encompassed the excellence specific to human beings as human beings. The question of how to be happy [was] the question of how to live well as a human being."

Today the word *happiness*, defined by *Merriam-Webster* (2018a)[28], refers to a "state of well-being and contentment, or a pleasurable and satisfying experience." It's certainly not bad for employees to experience their workplace as pleasurable, but let's face it: organizations exist for a host of other, larger purposes, which drive their behavior and processes far more profoundly than merely ensuring employee happiness. This is as it should be. Organizations, large and small, are created to meet a specific purpose (their mission), making them separate and distinct from the aggregate of individuals who work for them. Employment starts with the needs of the organization, and the needs of the employees come second. If there is no work to organize around, there is no need for shared work. In other words, where there is no employer, there is no employee.

Going back to our premise, then, that people make companies great, it's incumbent on every organization to ensure that the people who work there thrive, which is different from mere happiness, which is both transient and fleeting. Workers thrive in Bravespace workplaces. Sure, some days, we hope to feel pleasure and satisfaction at work. But when a worker solves a challenging problem or spends a long and difficult day at work, they lay their head down on their pillow at night, satisfied with their contribution, not because it made them happy, but because it mattered. Thriving at work invites many other human experiences beyond happiness: complexity, frustration, challenge, creativity, loss, confusion, inspiration, hope, and failure. What if we reframe the subject to be less about making sure that employees are happy, and more about whether they feel alive, are thriving, and feel sure what they're doing matters?

Real thriving at work, in any job, is about knowing that we're contributing to something bigger than ourselves. When we feel this, we're propelled to connect, produce, learn, listen, and contribute. It's the nuance of being human at work. We seek to feel seen, valued, and respected; when we don't, we become disheartened, unmotivated, and numb.

When leaders of any organization focus on making people happy, they might as well bring chocolate and beer to work; both of these cause short-term positive feelings, and temporary numbing. When leaders instead focus on facilitating ways in which every employee can thrive, they must dig deeper, beneath the surface, to reach what we as human beings need to function well. To help employees feel alive at work, leaders must look more closely and consider what motivates people, what makes their hearts sing, why they work, and what they dream.

Professors Andre Spicer and Carl Cederström (2015)[29] address the nuance of oversimplifying worker motivations to simple happiness: "We think there is a strong case for rethinking our expectation that work should always make us happy. It can be exhausting, make us overreact, drain our personal life of meaning, increase our vulnerability, and make us more gullible, selfish, and lonely. Most striking is that consciously pursuing happiness can drain the sense of joy we usually get from the really good things we experience."

Days in a job are made joyous in part by the contrast with the dark and difficult ones. Let's stop talking about happiness and focus on helping each other feel alive at work—bringing our huffing, puffing, thinking, sweating, engaging, arguing, stubborn, and brilliant selves to work in a way that matters far more than mere happiness.

Work is Work, but the Times They are a-Changin'

When I was young, my parents asked me to do chores around the house. I would whine and moan about it, as most kids do, no matter how easy or hard the task. My mom would say, "Well, they don't call it work for nothing!" Our work is supposed to cause us to sweat and strive; the word *work* describes an activity or effort toward a specific result. Academics and researchers have examined the complexities of what happens when people work together in organizations since the industrial revolution, which marked a massive migration from an agrarian society to an industrialized one. It was then that people moved to urban areas and congregated in companies for mass production and the efficiency impossible in the quilted fabric of farms across the nation.

As early as the late 1800s, Max Weber (1958)[30] wrote about his concern that the Industrial Revolution's focus on efficiency constrained employees to a kind of prison and "stripped a worker of their individuality." In the years since, development, organizational behavior, and organizational psychology have advanced theories of what it takes to harness the best people have to offer at work to benefit the company and, ultimately, society at large.

The intersection of what's good for people and what's good for business contains numerous paradoxes for leaders and employees to navigate. For example, the paradox between what's good for the individual and what's good for the group; the paradox between profitability and work/life balance; the paradox between worker safety and efficiency; and the paradox between fair wages and owner income. Occupational stress, work's impact on families, ephemeral balance, employee wellness, productivity, and other elements of the effect of work on people remain fascinating, epitomized by the volume of articles, podcasts, books, and theories about how we work and what is best for us.

The modern workplace is in great flux. New productivity tools introduced each week that are supposed to help us get more work done faster. We're connected with colleagues worldwide via a multitude of devices are always on. The gig economy produces more and more independent workers with flexibility and choice but without employee benefits or job security. Companies merge and sell. These changes in the world of work have both positive and negative effects on people globally. Since people make companies great, and because people contribute more when they are thriving at work, it's helpful to consider trends that impact the creation of workplaces fit for human life. Cammie Dunaway and I (Carrick and Dunaway 2017)[31] outlined the following key trends in our book *Fit Matters*, and they remain relevant and timely today:

- **New and Ambiguous Roles.** New jobs appear every year that did not previously exist—Social Media Coordinator, Director of First Impressions, Growth Hacker, to name a few. In our technology-driven economy of service businesses, where information (data) rules, jobs morph in novel and unanticipated ways. Gone are the days when selecting one career path in a known profession (doctor, lawyer, civil servant) was a sure thing for life. And even in known professions, paths are changing quickly; for example, physicians can review MRIs from thousands of miles away without seeing the patient, and marketers may work only in digital media realms. And this pace will increase; it's estimated that 65% of jobs will be available when today's kindergartners' graduate college don't exist today (Rosen 2011)[32].

- **Increase in the Desire for Meaning.** The days when a job was just to make money to provide for the family have passed; the purpose behind our desire to work has shifted. New workers (especially the Millennial generation) increasingly seek meaning when looking for a job. Despite the perks, promotions, pathways, or professions of a particular role, if employees can't find a higher purpose in their work or company, they'll feel disconnected, disenfranchised, and, ultimately, misfit. While this may have always been so, it feels more acute today when long-term employer-employee relationships are not a given. Most people can expect to have 11 to 13 jobs during their lifetimes.

- **Flexibility as a Currency.** Workers today aren't satisfied with traditional nine-to-five work hours; they prefer to schedule their work around hobbies, caregiving, and lifestyle choices. This dynamic alters the conventional construct of an office, where people sit in cubicles or meeting rooms and crank out documents and information. People want portability and flexibility in the way they work.

- **Information Overload.** Today the availability of data isn't an issue; we're swimming in information every minute of the day, accessible by various devices and from locations as wide-ranging as a boat in the Arctic to our neighborhood Starbucks. Access to information isn't an issue; the issue is knowing what information to pay attention to, and whether that information is relevant to our decision-making process.

- **Distributed Companies and Teams.** Digital connection anywhere, anytime, means that people and work are no longer organized in traditional settings. People work across platforms, time zones, languages, and cultures more than ever before, increasing demand for communication, clarity, and team cohesion. This trend puts pressure on employees at all levels to build social capital with people in all directions to get things done. It's feasible and likely that you have a boss or teammates you never actually see in person because they live across an ocean.

- **Speed.** Things happen faster than ever in the world of work today, resulting in increased stress and pressure for workers to quickly assimilate vast volumes of data. They make decisions fast for fear of falling behind or missing an opportunity. The internalized pressure to do more with less, in half the time, adds up to a head-down, shoulders-bunched, running-in-place iconoclastic image of American workers—all action, very little reflection.

- **Cloud Workers/Outsourcing.** An increasing number of workers are freelancers, and companies frequently reduce costs by outsourcing work to part-time or occasional workers to avoid overhead (Nunberg 2016[33]. This combination provides flexibility, but it fails to deliver stability and predictability for workers, which impacts their ability to keep ahead of living expenses, plan for big life events, and take advantage of company benefits. This trend has implications for the social contract between employer and employee in terms of long-term security, which affects individuals, families, and communities.

- **Sustainability Imperative.** Business growth for growth's sake is being replaced with purposeful, responsible growth in ways that minimize the impact on the environment, people, and natural resources. Greed is replaced by values, profit partners with impact, and business is increasingly leveraged as a force for good. The rise of social entrepreneurship means that more and more companies make money and make a difference. The new business status of benefit corporations, embraced by strong consumer brands such as Patagonia, Dansko, Method, and Ben & Jerry's, is evidence of the consumer's interest in products that, at a minimum, do not harm. This has implications for employees, particularly given their increasing desire for meaning and purpose at work.

- **Inclusion Imperative.** Numerous factors impact the extent to which organizations seek more diverse pools of workers. Having people with diverse experiences, views, and abilities makes companies more creative and innovative if they can navigate conflict. Beyond quotas and government regulations regarding equal employment opportunity, organizations increasingly seek workers representing their client populations. There are still challenges with the recruitment and retention of minorities (aka outsiders.) Still, the tide has turned when it comes to an interest in and commitment to diversity and, even more importantly, inclusion.

- **Overwhelmed Workers.** Lightning-fast changes in global markets have created an overwhelmed workforce. The popularity of yoga, meditation, and mindfulness exercises shows that we hunger for relief from feeling overloaded, inundated, and overstretched with the vast quantities of information and work demands we face day after day. Brigid Schulte (2014)[34] writes of both the costs of our work-hard culture to human beings as well as ways to reclaim our lives together.

- **Generational Turnover.** Baby boomers are entering retirement, and more than a third of the workforce (an estimated 56 million Americans) consisted of Millennials in 2017 (Cilluffo and Cohn 2017)[35]. The transfer of power, knowledge, experience, authority, and influence is well underway, and will undoubtedly continue to change how we work. Millennial workers motivated by priorities that are different from those of previous generations, and they're changing how work unfolds.

- **New and Evolving Rules for Managing.** The command and control management approaches of old are no longer de rigueur. California's Silicon Valley firms and those from other innovation hubs continue to establish paradigm-shifting ways to organize and motivate people at work, redefining what it means to manage and lead. From successfully flat structures where everyone is paid the same to team-based approaches where no one is the boss, the question of what will work is wide open. This trend impacts the relationships between bosses and employees and between employees and each other.

New World of Work = New Definition

In the face of these shifting sands, how do we determine what people need to perform well at work and to thrive as human beings?

We know what it takes to create circumstances at work that breed inspiration, performance, creativity, love, and delight. And yet we fail to do what it takes, time after time, leaving human beings at work disengaged, disenfranchised, angry, frustrated, and leaving the best they have to offer at home.

When work is good, our very human needs of work are met, at least in part. Workplaces that pay attention to fulfilling these needs are fit for human life. They are Bravespace workplaces. When these needs are fulfilled, we can do it all. We can use our bodies to engage in hard, manual labor. We can create beauty or design items that inspire and delight. We can talk to people and get them to do amazing things together. We can innovate. We can apply our knowledge, training, and skills to a task. We can build things. We can negotiate. We can sell. We can heal others. We can serve food.

The list of what we can do at and through work is limitless when we get what we need from work.

When work is good, we bring out our absolute best. Our best is our greatest chance to get results, meet our mission, and improve the world.

Endnotes

27 Aristotle. 2011. *Aristotle's Nicomachean Ethics.* Translated by Robert C. Bartlett and Susan D. Collins. Chicago: The University of Chicago Press.

28 Merriam-Webster. 2018a. S.v. "happiness." accessed November 9, 2018, https://www.merriam-webster.com/dictionary/happiness.

29 Spicer, André, and Carl Cederström. 2015. "The Research We've Ignored About Happiness at Work," *Harvard Business Review* (July 21). https://hbr.org/2015/07/the-research-weve-ignored-about-happiness-at-work.

30 Weber, Max. 1958. *The Protestant Ethic and the Spirit of Capitalism.* Translated by Talcott Parsons. New York: Charles Scribner's Sons.

31 Carrick, Moe, and Cammie Dunaway. 2017. *Fit Matters: How to Love Your Job.* Palmyra, VA: Maven House.

32 Rosen, Rebecca J. 2011. "Project Classroom: Transforming Our Schools for the Future." *The Atlantic* (August 29). http://www.theatlantic.com/technology/archive/2011/08/project-classroom-transforming-our-schools-for-the-future/244182/.

33 Nunberg, Geoff. 2016. "Goodbye Jobs, Hello 'Gigs': How One Word Sums Up a New Economic Reality." *National Public Radio* (January 11). http://www.npr.org/2016/01/11/460698077/ goodbye-jobs-hello-gigs-nunbergs-word-of-the-year-sums-up-a-new-economic-reality.

34 Schulte, Brigid. 2014. *Overwhelmed: Work, Love, and Play When No One Has the Time.* New York: Sarah Crichton Books.

35   Cilluffo, Anthony and D'Vera Cohn. 2017. "10 Demographic Trends Shaping the U.S. and the World in 2017." *FactTank: News in the Numbers* (April 27). Pew Research Center. http://www. pewresearch.org/fact-tank/2017/04/27/10-demographic-trends-shaping-the-u-s-and-the-world-in-2017/.

CHAPTER 6

Instructions
for Human Beings

*People need to be encouraged. People need to be reminded of
how wonderful they are. People need to be believed in—told
that they are brave and smart and capable of accomplishing all
the dreams they dream and more. Remind each other of this.*

—Stacey Jean Speer

When my children were young, their dad and I used to talk
about how we wished they had come with instruction books
with descriptions of what we should do in certain situations:

- What exactly is the time limit for letting him cry himself
  to sleep when each second seems like a lifetime of pain?
- What's the best way to compliment her beauty without
  making it the most important thing to her?
- When they won't sleep, but you feel like you'll die if *you*
  don't sleep, what's the best approach for dealing with it?

But, alas, we're not born with a guide. Humans are complex in
our motivations, our emotional reactions, our ways of thinking, our fears, and our stories. And when we get to be of working age, guess what? We bring all that complexity and diversity
right smack dab into the workplace.

As we discussed earlier, we have seven needs that work should fulfill. In this chapter, we'll explore these needs and construct a playbook for how employers can meet the needs of their employees at work. I ask employers to meet employee needs not only because it's the right thing to do, it feels good, or it makes people happy. My lived and professional experience points to one key reason why employers must understand and strive to meet the needs of their employees at work: it is the fastest way to get the results they seek. Ensuring that employees thrive at work means they bring their best talents to work every day, which improves business results and organizational value. After all, people make companies great.

"People problems" are the most-cited reason that organizations call me. The problem is invariably with a particular person or between particular people. In our assessment phase, we hear about the specific dynamics of Tom, Andrea or whoever is causing or contributing to the problem. Many clients have said to me, "This would be easy if it weren't for the people." Ah, yes.

Someone who calls us is usually looking for a) hope—if they could have solved this on their own, they surely would have—and b) a playbook—how they can change or influence a particular person to get a better outcome. People are messy. We're complex, diverse, and hard to understand without spending time together and communicating. We have many needs, and we don't always know exactly what they are or how to meet them.

Most of us come to work wanting to do a good job. It's part of our identity and central to our sense of self, to feel competent and worthy in our lives, including our work. In my experience with thousands of people in many workplaces over the years, I rarely meet people who purposefully want to do a bad job. We don't mean to cause problems at work, but we get all tangled up.

While writing *Fit Matters* with my co-author Cammie Dunaway, I was amazed whenever we talked to someone about work fit, they had a story about jobs they'd loved or hated. The stories about the jobs they'd loved always sounded like stories about a fun family picnic. When we asked what they loved about their job, they said things such as:

- "I just feel that people care about me here."
- "It's fun to come to work every day!"
- "I can't imagine working with a boss I respect more!"
- "I've looked for this job my whole career."

These were the best conversations, although they were rare. In book research and my consulting practice over the last 30-plus years, most stories I've heard are of misery:

- "I can't wait to get out of this job."
- "I'm looking for another job—this one sucks."
- "The time goes so slowly at work every day."
- "Does my boss think I'm an idiot?"

With *Fit Matters*, Cammie and I attempted to foster hope for people that work didn't have to suck the life out of them. We offered tools and practical approaches for people seeking new jobs to help them find their ideal setting and for people already in a job to craft their way to more positive experiences at work. We wanted to give employees the power to find fit rather than leaving it up to chance.

Repeatedly since *Fit Matters* came out, feedback about the framework we offered for work fit has been positive. In conversations with people and in reviews of the book, we repeatedly hear that the six elements we introduced capture what people are looking for in a job. Here are the six elements that determine whether an employee is likely to thrive at work:

- **Meaning Fit** is great when you feel that what you do matters.
- **Job Fit** is great when the responsibilities of your job align with your talents and provide growth opportunities.
- **Culture Fit** is great when your values and beliefs are compatible with the practices of your employer.
- **Relationship Fit** is great when you like and respect the people you work with and receive appropriate support and trust to do your job.
- **Lifestyle Fit** is great when your life outside work is supported by your employer's policies and practices.
- **Financial Fit** is great when you feel that you're paid fairly and when what your employer offers (salary, bonus, benefits, perks, and allowances) meets your needs.

Our research pointed to the fact that work fit always requires a trade-off—there is no perfect fit—and it's temporally sensitive, meaning that our needs change throughout our lives, and what we need at one stage of our careers may not be what we need in another. By thinking about the six elements of work fit, we can evaluate the opportunities we seek, whether it's a new job or to modify our current work situation to strengthen the match between what we, as unique individuals, need at work and what our employer offers.

For employers, the considerations of the six elements of work fit are more complicated, since redesigning your organization to fit each employee's needs is difficult.

I recommend designing the organization from the stripped-down, more essential needs that human beings bring to the workplace: the seven needs that work should fulfill. Ironically, designing a company to be fit for human life by consciously meeting the needs of the people who work there isn't always intuitive.

Can't We Just Do the Work?

I can't count the number of leaders I've had to convince that the work we would do together would impact their company's bottom line. They listen to me with faces of incredulity, doubt, and skepticism. And yet, invariably, when they experience the work, whether in the realm of leadership, team, culture, or conflict, they feel the benefit, and we never have to repeat that conversation. Though they're hard to measure, the ephemeral elements of being a Bravespace workplace are tangibly felt.

For example, I once worked with a very charismatic leader. And his company got results. But when the wheels started to come off the bus of his company, he became irritable with me. "Moe, I hear that people are (insert descriptive negative state of being here), but this is, after all, a business. Right? It's not summer camp."

His company had more than double the average employee turnover (21%). And the exit interviews revealed deep problems. People commented, "I don't need to come to work every day afraid my manager is going to publicly humiliate me." "My husband threatens to divorce me because I work every evening and weekend, and we have little kids." I answered this CEO with words I have said many times, "You're right; it's 'just work.'" And then I asked him a question I knew he would get, "What will happen if you have to rehire 20% of your employees every year just to stay even?" Ka-ching!— money talks.

Any group is only as fast as its slowest member. Companies require people to do the jobs to be done. People need Bravespace workplaces to do their best work or they'll leave. Either actually or mentally, the only thing more expensive than an employee leaving is an employee who is miserable and stays.

Work is not meant to be summer camp. But people need to thrive while working; when they do, it's good for business. By *thrive,* I mean and *Merriam-Webster* (2018b)[36] agrees more than just survive or get by but to "grow vigorously, to prosper, to flourish." Most of us have, at some point in our lives, had that job that's just feeding us, a position where we were marking time. But the jobs where we thrive can elevate any mundane work situation, and work is good.

When I traveled in Rwanda with a client, I was assigned a young driver and guide, Moses, whom I adored (we had many hours together during several trips). His hours were long, his pay low. One hot, arduous travel day, I asked him why he stayed with the job given its difficulties. I remember his response so clearly: "I get to meet people from all over the world and help them see my country. I feel so lucky! I'm a good driver, and I think my boss knows that and cares about me."

It's not rocket science to understand what it takes to design and lead a workplace fit for human life, but it's not easy, either. People are diverse, needy, and complex. So, what do employees want from their employers? There are seven needs people have that work should fulfill:

- To meet our basic requirements – to make enough money or non-cash compensation to provide food, clothing, shelter, and safety
- To contribute – to do something that matters to someone
- To be seen – and known
- To connect – in fundamental ways, with other people
- To learn – and become better
- To feel supported – to be able to be brave, knowing that there are risks
- To make our lives work – to be able to do the things that matter to us and are ours to do

Some of these needs, such as pay, are obvious, and employees negotiate for them. But most peoples' other needs lurk within, neither named nor directly observable by their employers. People can't pinpoint what they need from work because these work needs are so basically connected to their essential needs as human beings that they don't differentiate them.

A study called the Grant Study is the longest-running studies on human development. This study has run since 1938, and it has followed 268 men who started as Harvard undergraduates, for 75 years. A study of this magnitude is valuable not only because of its duration, but also for its range. Data was collected on physical traits, family relationships, financial status, health, diet, habits, IQ, and much more. George Vaillant (2012)[37] was the director of the study for more than 30 years, and he published a summary of his insights. He cited seven significant factors that contribute to healthy aging and happiness. They are:

- Education
- Stable marriage
- Healthy weight
- Exercise
- Not smoking
- Not abusing alcohol
- Employing mature adaptations

He concluded that good social skills and coping methods are crucial to overall health and well-being. Still, the most telling aspect of the study came when the subjects' relationships and their life satisfaction were analyzed. There were direct links between having a warm relationship with a mother on the one hand and financial success, mental health in old age, and career effectiveness (among others) on the other. A warm relationship with a father manifested itself in a decreased likelihood of adult anxiety and an increased ability to play, as well as a general feeling of happiness.

Valiant's final thought is remarkable for all who feel on an elusive quest for happiness. He finished by saying that the Grant Study points to a straightforward, five-word conclusion: "Happiness is love. Full stop."

Relationships Are the Key to Happiness at Work, as in Life

We cannot achieve happiness at work without warm relationships. Happiness is developing relationships and the moments we connect as people. The most essential ingredient for what we need at work is fruitful, connected relationships. For any organization with employees, a focus on healthy relationships at work is essential. You might be nodding your head right now, saying, "duh." I know, it seems so easy. But in truth, we experience our company primarily through our immediate supervisor, so our relationship with that person is critical to whether we thrive. No matter how accessible and connecting the CEO or owner is, if the person we directly work for alienates us, we experience work negatively.

Warm and healthy relationships at work require trust and self-awareness; both are big subjects that we'll tackle in Chapter 8: Making Work Good. Until we get there, a good starting place for bringing out the best in the people who work for you is to focus time, energy, and effort on knowing yourself. Warren Bennis, a leadership development theorist and advocate, said, "The leader never lies to himself, especially about himself, knows his flaws as well as his assets, and deals with them directly."[38]

Instructions for Human Beings

Let's review what people need from work in more detail and reflect on relevant questions that any leader or business owner should be prepared to answer. Human beings (including the ones who work for you) need these things from you and your organization, no matter if your organization is big or small, private or public, in business, healthcare, education, or any other sector:

- **People need money to meet their basic requirements.** This means that you need to think about how you plan to pay them and what currencies you'll offer in addition to pay. In my hometown of Bend, Oregon, employers consider offering time off during workdays so that employees can enjoy the outdoor playground we live in. From mountain biking on fall afternoons to being the first to ski Mt. Bachelor early on Monday mornings, a currency that matters here, in addition to pay, is the chance to play. *Are you paying fairly? Are you looking beyond pay for what matters to your people? Can people meet their basic needs on what you pay them? What can you offer in addition to money?*

- **People need to do something that matters to someone; they need to contribute.** This means that we need to be able to connect the dots between what we do and something bigger. Every job, from the front line to the most senior executive, exists for a reason. Mark worked on the line for a speaker manufacturer, and he said that he loved his job despite the tedious nature of the work, because he knew that he was helping people listen to beautiful music, which made their hearts sing. *Are you spending time with your employees to connect the dots between what they do daily and the benefit or impact of that work on someone else? Are you coaching your leaders to spend time doing the same?*

- **People need to feel seen, not anonymous.** Being seen means being known. It means that the people we work for and with know our name, and they know what our job is. They notice if we come to work and are joyous or down. Recently a CEO client and I were on a walking coaching session, and we bumped into an employee. The employee knew the CEO right away, and when the CEO recognized him and asked how things were going, it was like watching the sun rise. The employee felt valued and seen because his boss's boss knew who he was and cared how he was. *Do you know who works for you by name? Do you spend the time necessary to get to know them in small but vital ways?*

- **People need to connect with other people via real connection.** This is what the Grant Study shows and what Brené Brown's research illuminates: we are hard-wired for connection, and need it as much as we need water. This goes beyond company teambuilding and beer on Fridays; it has everything to do with whether your organization facilitates and supports the process of forming human connections. The best way to do this is by being genuine and human, admitting your mistakes or admitting that you don't know. Nothing, and I mean nothing, draws others closer to us than small acts of vulnerability that reveal our humanity. *Are you showing your employees what's under the hood? Do you support small intervals in time when the explicit purpose is human connection?*

- **People need to learn and grow.** The need to learn is so basic that in our first book, *Fit Matters*, Cammie and I offered it as an overriding seventh element that encompasses all six work fit elements. We want to become better, to challenge our thinking and being in various ways. *As an employer, are you aware of what an employee might want to learn with you? And are you talking about it with them? How are people able to grow or learn at your organization?*

- **People need to feel, and be, safe and supported.** Google's germinal 2015 Aristotle Project validated what many of us already knew: members of high-performing groups at work have psychological safety between them. Psychological safety is "a sense of confidence that the team will not embarrass, reject, or punish someone for speaking up," according to Harvard Business School professor Amy Edmondson (1999)[39]. "It describes a team climate characterized by interpersonal trust and mutual respect in which people are comfortable being themselves." This includes being able to feel like you belong, even when differences (race, gender, physical ability, nationality, sexual orientation, and more) could make you feel like an outsider. *Do your employees feel safe enough to speak up? Do you spend time and effort to creating an environment in which listening to each other, and showing sensitivity to feelings and needs, is valued? Do you practice inclusion and model it in* *your organization, exploring your own unconscious biases and systematic advantages?*

- **People need to be able to make their lives work.** We lead divergent and varied lives. What works for one person may not work for another. Some companies focus on professional athletes as employees because athletes need flexible hours to train, and they need the income. Others make work hours appropriate for working parents. Obviously your organization needs to do what it needs to do, which may mean that employees must flex how, when, or where they work. But a single parent will likely need to be home by a certain time. Or if an employee you value does her best thinking between 7 a.m. and 9 a.m., can you facilitate the end of her shift to be 3 p.m. rather than 5 p.m. so that she can take advantage of her best thinking time without overworking? We can't completely design workplaces around employees, of course, but if employees can't make their lives work around our organizational needs, they won't. *Do you pay attention to the ways in which your workplace supports and enlivens your employees? Do you act in ways that are consistent with the values you profess?*

As we reviewed in Chapter 2, The US Surgeon's Generals Report reveals complete and comprehensive inclusion of these seven needs of work in its framework supporting engines of well-being.

The Surgeon General's Framework for Workplace Mental Health and Well-Being[40]

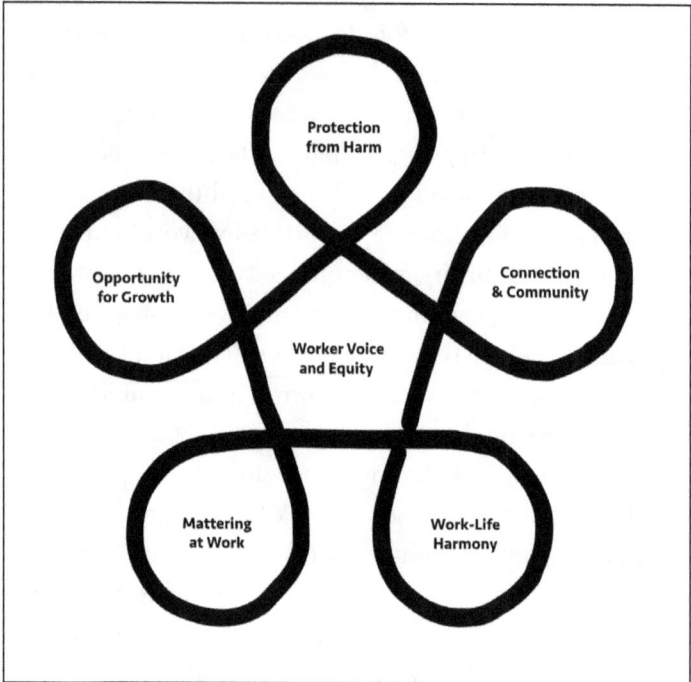

Protection from Harm

Opportunity for Growth

Connection & Community

Worker Voice and Equity

Mattering at Work

Work-Life Harmony

The Bravespace Workplace Framework for Thriving at Work overlaid with the Surgeon General's 2023 Report on Workplace Mental Health and Well-Being

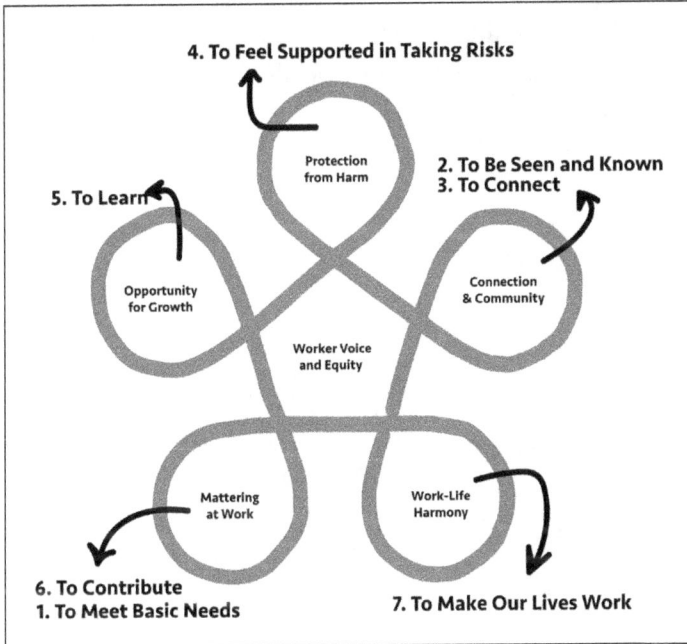

4. To Feel Supported in Taking Risks

Protection from Harm

2. To Be Seen and Known
3. To Connect

5. To Learn

Connection & Community

Opportunity for Growth

Worker Voice and Equity

Mattering at Work

Work-Life Harmony

6. To Contribute
1. To Meet Basic Needs

7. To Make Our Lives Work

The Bravespace Workplace Framework

7 Human Needs From Work

1. To Meet Basic Needs
2. To be Seen and Known
3. To Connect
4. To be Supported in Taking Risks
5. To Learn
6. To Contribute
7. To Make Our Lives Work

If you own or manage a company, keep in mind, with everything you do, what people need from work. The reasons that we work are complex, and often beneath the surface, but they are consistent for most of us. By designing every facet of your workplace around the needs of people, you'll create a Bravespace workplace where workers can do their best work for and with you.

Endnotes

36 Merriam-Webster. 2018b. S.v. "thrive." accessed September 29, 2018, https://www.merriam-webster.com/dictionary/thrive.

37 Vaillant, George E. 2012. *Triumphs of Experience.* Cambridge, MA: Belknap Press.

38 Bennis, Warren. 2009. *On Becoming A Leader*, 4th Edition. New York: Basic Books.

39 Amy Edmondson. 1999. "Psychological Safety and Learning Behavior in Work Teams." *Administrative Science Quarterly* 44 (2): 350–83.

40 https://www.hhs.gov/surgeongeneral/priorities/workplace-well-being/index.html

CHAPTER 7

The Hard Stuff IS the Soft Stuff

Emotional labor is not invisible work or unpaid chores. It's when a job requires you to show or hide emotions—flight crews staying calm, teachers showing passion, nurses showing compassion. It's as vital as physical and cognitive labor.

—Adam Grant

Authentic has become a widely overused word today. I've seen it used to train customer service reps who plaster fake smiles on their faces and ask, "How's your day going?" when they couldn't care less. Authentic is added to descriptions of furniture, clothes, and hotel rooms to connote *original* when the product is a newly made *copy* of something original. And it's used to train leaders at all levels on how to act with their employees in ways that garner trust and partnership.

I find it ironic that another retail term for *authentic* is *distressed*, as in "distressed denim" and "distressed cabinet," which are used as selling points to show that the item has some fraying around the edges. It doesn't look freshly minted right off the factory floor, which makes it appear to us more friendly, warm, and "real." When human beings are authentic (real) as Margery Williams (1922)[41] said so poignantly in the children's book classic *The Velveteen Rabbit*, they're easier to love. The problem is that the word's overuse has strained its meaning, making interactions at times palpably artificial. Like the made-up things around us, we sometimes mimic others in a way that, despite our intentions, allows others to sense that we're not our authentic selves.

Being Real

An essential element of Bravespace workplaces is the presence of authentic expressions of humanity and human nature. *Remember, a Bravespace workplace is one in which people can show up as they are, both worthy and flawed, and do great things together.* Rather than being carte blanche for people to wear their bathrobes to work and blurt out their thoughts at the expense of others, being real at work means something completely different. What being real means is unique to each one of us. We know it in our gut when someone shows up authentically, and we can sense when someone is faking it. No amount of reading, training, or degrees can guarantee that we'll capably be true and authentic with others at work. Being real with one another at work requires stripping away the protective layers that keep our feelings, opinions, and tensions hidden. Decades of politically correct, ingrained ways of being at work must be put aside to discover the unique, true, and honest story we bring to work every day. There are seven practices for being real at work:

- **Walk your talk.** The fastest way to erode trust is to espouse one thing and do another. We tune in to one another at work based on what we see done, not what's promised. A client of mine was the general manager of a company. He told his team that family needs come first, so they should prioritize their families regarding work-related impacts such as overtime and weekend interruptions. During a regularly scheduled meeting, one of the directors asked the GM if he had expected a response to his email, sent at 5 a.m. on the Sunday before the meeting. The director had seen the email when he came to work, hadn't read it, and worried that his boss expected an answer by the time they met Monday. The subtext of their conversation was, "You say you want us to prioritize family, but you consistently work evenings and weekends. This tells me that you also expect me to, despite what you say." To their credit, this was a fruitful conversation. The GM openly owned his own working style and acknowledged that his direct reports might interpret his behavior as contradicting his words. They agreed that there were times when it was essential to go the extra mile, but these instances should be exceptions and not the rule given, what they valued.

Being real

"Real isn't how you are made," said the Skin Horse. "It's a thing that happens to you. When a child loves you for a long, long time, not just to play with, but REALLY loves you, then you become Real."

"Does it hurt?" asked the Rabbit.

"Sometimes," said the Skin Horse, for he was always truthful. "When you are Real you don't mind being hurt."

"Does it happen all at once, like being wound up," he asked, "or bit by bit?"

"It doesn't happen all at once," said the Skin Horse. "You become. It takes a long time. That's why it doesn't happen often to people who break easily, or have sharp edges, or who have to be carefully kept. Generally, by the time you are Real, most of your hair has been loved off, and your eyes drop out and you get loose in the joints and very shabby. But these things don't matter at all, because once you are Real you can't be ugly, except to people who don't understand."

—Margery Williams, *The Velveteen Rabbit*

- **Name the ugly, scary, and hard.** The most common behavioral problem I see in workplaces is the reluctance of people to dig into unsavory, challenging, and painful conversations. There are resources to help people navigate conflict, give feedback, and have difficult but crucial conversations, but instead, we often avoid those difficult interactions. There are many reasons why we don't have the hard conversations we need to: fear, insecurity, concern about hurting another, identity, shame, perfectionism, positional authority, fear of recrimination, risk, and more. But here's the thing: a Bravespace workplace is built on honesty, honesty that's kind and compassionate. For nearly a century, management practice has scrubbed feelings out of workplaces as if they're dirty. But Bravespace workplaces are built upon the recognition that feelings are essential elements of the workplace that we must work through together.

I once had a client who was preparing to announce layoffs to the employees who remained. Initially, his talk was composed mostly of data and numbers that gave the context of his decisions. But the reality was that he was sad and hurt that the company had to lay off people, including some of his friends, to survive. His decision to start his presentation by sharing his sadness at the layoffs had the opposite effect of what he expected. He was worried about appearing weak, but his tenderness and tears reassured others. They felt sad and lost as well, and by naming the dark part of the process, he cleared the way for everyone to understand why the changes had to happen and what was necessary going forward. We must always tell the truth about the hard stuff, with care, kindness, and compassion.

- **You're the leader; you go first.** Employees copy leaders. They tune in to what their leader does to determine what they should be doing. Remember that whenever you act.

Years ago, I sailed across the Pacific with a small crew. I was on night watch, in the Pacific Ocean when we hit something. I alerted the crew and the captain, who came topside. My pulse and my panic were racing. "Have we damaged the hull?" "Should I lower the sails?" "Where's the life raft?" When I saw the captain, I noticed his calm demeanor. He quietly listened. He called down below to the others, "Does anyone see or hear water below?" He adjusted the sails to get us on course and off the accidental jibe we had done. I felt my panic subside. I firmly held the wheel and started going through the checklist in my head. Without being aware of it and without any direction from the captain, I had begun to internalize his reactions and demeanor and make them my own. He knew more than I did about things that bump in the night in the wild open ocean, and his calm moves informed mine. As leaders, we must go first toward creating a Bravespace workplace. What we do, others will copy.

- **Remember, there are no guarantees.** People ask me how they can trust others if they have no proof of trustworthiness. They're looking for proof, wondering, "If I lean into you, open my heart to you, show you my unformed ideas, share my input with you, will I be safe? Or will something bad happen?"

We're alert for the things that threaten our feelings of security and our identity: Will you insult me?

Diminish me? Will you tell me no? Will you keep my secret? Will you tell me the truth? Will you leave me? Will this hurt?

At work, just as in life, there's no guarantee. We may feel hurt, diminished, insulted, or alienated at work; or even fired. These are the risks of living. Every day, we face rejection and loneliness as we take the chance to make friends and to love. We form connection and meaning at work through the presence and practice of vulnerability, which Brené Brown describes as uncertainty, risk, and emotional exposure. At work our sense of self-worth is most vulnerable—"Am I worthy and competent here?"

Most of us come to work wanting to do a good job and be worthy. Brown (2012)[42] says, "Vulnerability is not weakness, and the uncertainty, risk, and emotional exposure we face daily are not optional. Our only choice is a question of engagement. Our willingness to own and engage with our vulnerability determines the depth of our courage and the clarity of our purpose; the level to which we protect ourselves from being vulnerable is a measure of our fear and disconnection." There are no guarantees that our courage in contributing to a Bravespace workplace will be rewarded, but the only alternative is to opt out and work independently and in isolation. When we work with others there's no guarantee that it will all work out, but we must show up anyway. The hard parts of work make the sweet parts even sweeter.

- **Remember that it all made sense at the time.** In the context of Bravespace workplaces, it's easy to look in the rearview mirror and find blame, shame, or recrimination for the mistakes we or others have made. We tell ourselves things like "They never should've hired him," or "This will never work," or "How did they mess it up *this* badly?" When we do this we waste time and effort assigning blame rather than using that time and effort to create solutions for moving forward together. My favorite mantra, "It all made sense at the time," profoundly eases the feelings of blame and recrimination we feel when we look at our past actions.

Every day, people make decisions in the best way they know how according to their present knowledge. We don't know what we don't know. We proceed toward action without surety or completeness. If we remember that a decision of the past made sense at the time (for the people who made it), we spend less time obsessing about our past actions and are more able to move forward with grace and forgiveness.

- **Use self-compassion as evidence of empathy.** When I make a mistake, the things I say in the privacy of my mind are astounding. I would never say them to a friend or an employee:
  o "How could you be so stupid?"
  o "What on earth were you thinking?"
  o "You shouldn't be surprised this turned out badly; you are a loser."
  o "What made you think you could do this?"

When I look at my imperfections, I often become negative, hostile, judgmental, and shaming toward myself. It doesn't help me, and it doesn't help others. When we treat leaders as people who can and should do things perfectly, we risk creating disconnection and eroding trust. In our deficit-oriented, results-focused business culture, accountability often looks like this kind of self-recrimination.

When leaders focus on their weaknesses and verbally abuse themselves for being less than perfect, they demonstrate to those around them that they lack compassion and empathy. It's the human condition to learn from our mistakes, so more mistakes mean more learning. Exhibiting self-compassion to those around us indicates that we have an accurate sense of self as both worthy and flawed and that we see mistakes, including our own, as opportunities to learn. We model empathy and move on. What helps others is to know that we're capable of having compassion during difficulty including our own, and we believe a solution or remediation is possible.

- **Own your sh*t.** I was interviewing clients for a structure project recently. The group of fifteen employees told me that their boss was toxic to the whole team. I shared the anonymous feedback with the boss, who became visibly upset. He said, "How can these people afford the time to whine and complain about me to you? This goes to show you—they're incompetent and lazy." Hmmmm. Surely, the employee group contributed to the team's eroded trust. Still, when fifteen people report to a neutral third party that the boss's mean and negative behavior is demoralizing them, it's wise to be at least curious about it. Better yet, own it.

I wished for this leader that he had recognized his employees' pain as real and that he had empathized. Then he could have become genuinely interested in how others saw him and why they said those things. The perception that others had about his impact was terrific information about what changes he could and should make to his leadership practice. Had the leader owned up to how he came across, recognizing that his positive intention hadn't reached its audience, he might have shown his team that he wanted to lead them and that he was willing to learn.

Some ways he could have done this include being curious about his reaction to their feedback. He could have asked questions such as, "Why am I so negative?" "Why am I disappointed?" "What needs to happen with the group?" If he had asked himself reflective questions such as these, he could have learned about himself, which would have helped him to lead differently and to impact his company positively.

The Soft Stuff

Often when I describe to people what I do, they call it "the soft stuff," which implies work that focuses on people but is disconnected from the business. There is a tendency in business to emphasize a measurable return on investment in people and organizational development. I get it—we want to know if the effort and expense make a difference. The fact is, it's hard, if not impossible, to measure whether our actions about people have the impact we want, where we want it. As a CEO once said to me, "I can't measure in dollars and cents whether our work on culture here has made our company better single-handedly, but I can sure tell you that it has had a positive impact qualitatively." When we do the right thing for people, we know it, and it feels right. When we don't, it doesn't.

People make companies great, which means that the great companies of tomorrow are the ones that will attract people to work for and with them and that the quality of those workplaces will encourage people to flourish. That quality will be maintained in these same Bravespace workplaces so that the people who work there continue to thrive.

Leaders everywhere are under increasing pressure to deliver results while fostering trust and connection with their teams.

It can feel like an impossible task to lead well and manage your workload.

To help you succeed in building trust and connection, you should stop doing these three things in your one-on-ones immediately.

- Stop avoiding emotions.
- Stop jumping to solutions.
- Stop trying to lead people with a one-size-fits all approach.

Stop Avoiding Emotions

It's understandable to feel uncomfortable with feelings in the workplace, but avoiding emotions denies your team the opportunity to build emotional connection. When we ignore the emotions that underpin behavior, it can lead to a lack of trust, a lack of open dialogue, and a lack of understanding that it's ok to make mistakes.

Stop Jumping to Solutions

I, too, was trained to solve problems. I like solving problems because it feels good, they need to be solved, and I get praised for it.

But you need to stop.

When you jump to solutions, you aren't allowing your team the opportunity to come up with solutions. It sends the message that they can't solve their own problems, which can be demotivating and discouraging.

Stop trying to lead with a one-size-fits-all-approach

Policies, guidelines, and practices are helpful to enforce a minimum standard of compliance.

But you can't lead everyone the same way.

Leading people with a one-size-fits all approach will only lead to frustration and disengagement. Everyone is different and has different needs, and as a result, creating connection requires recognizing people's uniqueness.

Take the time to get to know each individual on your team and tailor your approach to meet their needs.

What to do instead

Now that you know what to stop doing, here's what you should be doing instead:

- **Listen**. Listen to understand rather than to come up with a solution.
- **Connect**. Connect with your team on an emotional level. Show people that they can trust you.

- **Encourage**. Encourage your team to take risks and to think outside of the box.
- **Support**. Support your team in their efforts to come up with solutions to the problems they face in their job.

These key actions are embedded in a practice we teach called, The Heart Habit. This simple tool is a counterbalance to the head habits that leaders are so often required to bring—their knowledge, ideas, experience, and intellect.

The Heart Habit
The Heart Habit is a practice of developing the skills to recognize, understand, and leverage emotions at work.

Practitioners of The Heart Habit understand that emotions aren't some untouchable, fear-able thing. Instead, they see emotions as a crucial data source about their world.

Equipped with this brave, accepting mindset, you can get back to work—instead of getting derailed by big feelings.

What it isn't
The Heart Habit is not about letting loose with unchecked emotionality at work.

It can be so tempting for leaders to fear that to work with emotions they have to turn their workplace into a counselor's office.

That's not at all what you want.

I'm not a therapist or a counselor; I'm a workplace expert. Rather than a dissertation on the neurobiology of emotion, The Heart Habit is about noticing and leveraging the emotions that are already happening.

Like any habit, The Heart Habit will require an investment of conscious energy before it becomes an automatic response.

It involves reflecting on feeling states, understanding and practicing empathy, gaining awareness of the underlying emotions behind common problems, understanding the landscape and normalized habits around emotions, and learning to internalize and practice the skills necessary to work with emotions.

The Heart Habit can become an automatic response to difficult emotions and situations at work through practice and repetition.

The Four Elements of The Heart Habit are:

1. Familiarize Emotion
2. Hold Space
3. Get Underneath the Real Problem
4. Normalize Habits

Step 1. Familiarize Emotion

Think about, notice, and get comfortable with emotions. The first step in developing The Heart Habit is to get comfortable with emotions. Here are some strategies to get started:

1. Affirm your capacity to feel. "I accept that I have emotions. I am willing to feel them."
2. Learn to notice emotions, in yourself and others.
3. Develop your language and vocabulary around emotions.

Remember that feelings are our physiological response to intense experiences such as perceived threats, and emotions are how we try to describe feelings in words. Feelings are common to the experience of being human in every culture. By getting to know your emotions and those of the people around you, you can start to develop a better understanding of the emotions that exist in the workplace.

Step 2. Hold Space

The second component of The Heart Habit is to hold and sit with the emotion that comes up at work, which means simply to hold space. What you want to communicate is that it's okay to have feelings and to share them. This is achieved by:

- Humble Inquiry
- Asking ambiguous, open-ended questions (see inset)
- Being aware of body language and tone of voice.

By expressing acceptance and emotional safety, you can create an environment where emotions can be explored and discussed openly and honestly. Holding space with empathy is essential for developing The Heart Habit.

Step 3. Get Underneath the Real Problem

There are several common symptoms leaders experience at work that **seem** like they're about work but are really about emotions.

For example:

Symptom	Problem	Common underlying emotions	Antidote
People don't get the feedback they need.	Without good feedback, they don't know how to improve.	Foreboding, defensiveness, resentment, worry, avoidance	Regular, clear, direct feedback (complimentary and learning-focused)
People don't tell their leader what is true for them	Leaders lose engagement through low trust.	Distrust, betrayal, isolation, anxiety, avoidance	Leaders get curious and regularly create space for real talk
People talk about each other, not to each other (gossip, triangulation)	Lack of courage and team health	Anxiety, frustration, fear, resentment, comparative shaming	Build teams who care
When things go wrong, the focus is on finger-pointing and blame	Poor accountability	Shame, anguish, betrayal, self-protection	Normalize learning, build an accountability culture

Step 4. Normalize The Heart Habit

Normalizing habits happens when we shed inherited constructs such as that emotions are bad or that rational thinking is the only relevant data source at work. We get distracted by the habit of being right, trying to win, productivity, and problem-solving, instead of noticing the feelings and resultant emotions. By making the critical nature of the feelings underpinning the problem a top priority, leaders model the courage to deal with hard things and resolve the issue between you.

The soft stuff of a workplace fit for human life inspires people to come to work, and stay once they get there. These workers contribute wisdom, energy, ideas, experience, talent, courage, and authority. They also bring their imperfect humanity, egos, past wounds, fears, insecurities, and complex needs to the workplace. We can't have the positives without the negatives, which means that leaders of the Bravespace workplaces of tomorrow will spend time, energy, effort, and resources to tend to the beautiful "soft stuff " that their people bring to work every day.

When work is good, we are fully seen for the messy, imperfect, unique humans that we are—diverse, complex, and awe-inspiring.

Endnotes

41   Williams, Margery. 1922. *The Velveteen Rabbit*. New York: George H. Doran Company.

42   Brown, Brené. 2012. *Daring Greatly: How the Courage to Be Vulnerable Transforms the Way We Live, Love, Parent, and Lead*. New York: Avery.

CHAPTER 8

Making Work Good

The plan is to fan this spark into a flame.

—Lin-Manuel Miranda

Making work good for people is simple.

Which doesn't mean it is easy.

The model I use has evolved over 30 years of consulting to hundreds of organizations and thousands of leaders. It is based on countless interviews, assessments, interventions, and research.

This model is practical and has risen from the brave organizations I've had the privilege of working with in my many years as a consultant, coach, facilitator, and speaker. My clients include the big names, the privately-owned, the publicly-held, nonprofits, school districts, agencies, and health care institutions. They range from under ten employees to more than 100k employees.

This approach is not theoretical.

It is tried and true, tested in the halls and walls of workplaces filled with regular leaders and average employees who sought to build cultures that activated their people's talents fully in order to serve the mission and make a profit.

The model to Make Work Good is about building bravespace workplaces for tomorrow. It incorporates the brilliant work of the many consultants, coaches, writers, and researchers who have come before me and shared their work with the world.

For all of your wisdom, I am grateful.

There are three critical elements to making work good by becoming a bravespace workplace, each outlined in the following chapters:

1. People Leadership
2. Conscious Brave Culture
3. Teams Who Care

Each section includes practical tips for everyone at work to take action: People Leaders, Employees, and People Experience/HR.

It doesn't matter where you start, just that you do.

Getting there is a process, not an event, and will require heart, hope, and honesty at every step.

You can do this.

Bravespace Workplace Framework

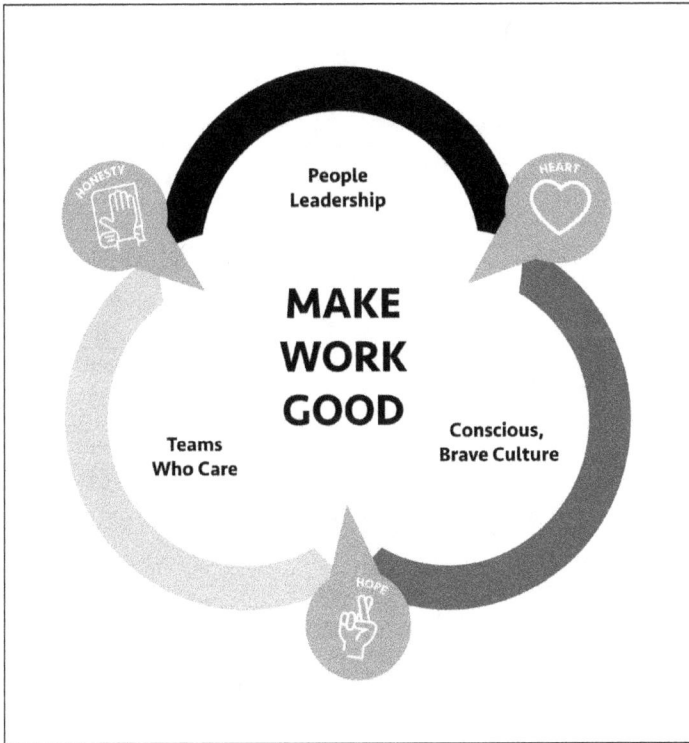

PART III

Invest in Leaders
Who are Good for People

CHAPTER 9

Connection

The acquisition of wealth is no longer the driving force of our lives. We work to better ourselves and the rest of humanity.

—Jean-Luc Picard

Our inherited notions of good People Leadership are built on outdated models from centuries ago. Leaders are taught to have all the answers, all of the time, and never let anyone see what is underneath excellence and performance.

These dated models of leadership says that a good leader…

- survives by focusing on the future and moving as quickly away from the past as possible;
- has immense capacity to stand alone, is resolute;
- never waivers in his can-do optimism;
- is motivated by the vague idea of "helping others";
- rewards hard work, action, and task completion exclusively;
- strives for perpetual growth;
- acts in moderation and quiet strength;
- values status and rank over connection.

Nothing is inherently wrong with this mindset—most of us benefit from utilizing these strengths at the right time and place!

And yet these traits are counterpoised against other, more prototypically "feminine" qualities that are increasingly urgently needed at work.

Researchers Michael D'Antonio and John Gerzema attest to this change—and the "feminization" of leadership—in their book *The Athena Doctrine: How Women (and the Men Who Think Like Them) Will Rule the Future*[43], they say, "All leaders, male or female, innately possess feminine qualities like empathy, candor, and vulnerability—the difference lies in which leaders choose to suppress those qualities and which choose to leverage them as strengths."

Julia Boorstin, in her recently released best-selling book, *When Women Lead*, reveals common traits from 60 women who have changed organizations and achieved incredible results with characteristics like high change resilience, deep empathy, vulnerability, gratitude as a practice, and incorporating diverse views that fill gaps left behind make counterparts for years.

Additionally, firms with female CEOs and CFOs produce superior stock price performance, compared to the market average, and firms with high gender diversity on their board of directors are more profitable and larger than firms with low gender diversity, according to a new study from S&P Global Market Intelligence.

Collectively, these data points add up to one clear message: our historical notions of what good People Leadership is are outdated. And new practices are required for leaders of all gender identities for results.

Our notions of good leadership mainly stem from the overseer model of the industrial revolution (imagine the long row of sewing machines and the boss with a whip in Les Misérables!) These included traits such as:

- Efficiency rules
- Rugged individualism
- Can-do attitude
- Motivations stemming from intellectual principles of conscience
- Focus on hard work, action, and task completion
- Striving for growth
- Measured moderation and quiet strength
- Status and rank over connection
- PROFIT as North Star

Multiple data sources and results tell us today that the traits that are called for the future are radically different:

- Ability to connect
- Clear and compassionate candor
- Empathy
- Willingness to be open and transparent
- Capacity for courage and vulnerability
- Humility as expressed in curiosity
- Patience
- Capacity to be trustworthy
- Able to flex and adapt to change
- Purpose as the driver of profit

The No-Heroes Journey

The change afoot is a movement away from our traditional notions of leaders as problem-solvers, fixers, and heroes who rule with directives and power using rationality over emotion. It is underlined by the burgeoning awareness that women at work (who continue to be under-represented in most upper echelon power roles) may have advantages in how they show up over how men have historically been trained by society to lead.

Joseph Campbell's classic book, *The Hero's Journey* (a long revered archetype, particularly resonant for men), gets debunked in the No-Heroes journey to People Leadership. Instead of the protagonist leaving his community to go on a quest for answers, being tempted by distractions, and then carrying his wisdom back to "the people" to bestow his genius ideas on everyone, the new paradigm for People Leadership is not of the hero on a white horse slaying dragons but rather a connected, humane leader who leverages the talents of all to do the hard things.

The American Psychological Association released guidelines for psychological practice for boys and men in 2018, the first research of its kind. It revealed "the traditional masculinity marked by stoicism, competitiveness, dominance, and aggression is, on the whole, harmful." Written over a period of 40 years, the report lays out striking health disparities between men and women including that men are five times as likely to die from suicide as women and are 50% and 80% more likely to die from heart disease and cancer respectively than women.

From where I sit, it is (way past) time we elevated the skills of emotional intelligence and human connection for everyone at work, especially leaders of people.

The landscape of work is changing right before our eyes.

- People won't tolerate jobs that leave them constantly burned out and exhausted.
- 81% of workers today report they'll be looking for work-places that **support mental health**.
- Most leaders consistently overestimate how employees are doing and how supported they feel.
- A massive 68% of workers reported **feeling actively disengaged**, meaning they're disgruntled and disloyal.
- Employers and employees disagree on whether remote and flexible work arrangements are good.

The person we work for (our immediate leader) is how we experience our company. Something needs to change.

Traditional education and organizational leadership programs fail to nurture People Leaders.

From business school to medical school, we consistently fail to provide the tools and skills People Leaders need to create meaningful connection, coaching, and support for human beings.

Business, healthcare, education, nonprofit, and other leaders are taught technical and analytical skills in their sector and, those skills are often how and why people are promoted. Great sales people become salesleaders. Excellent provider clinicians become medical directors. Skilled engineers become engineering managers.

This is what I call Performance Leadership, and those skills do matter.

But focusing on them alone is draining the life out of people, crippling our workforces. In the short term, Performance Leadership serves organizational and business interests by focusing on delivering results.

But Performance Leadership as a sole focus comes with a high cost to employees and employers, including burnout, disengagement, poor health, job misery, and other toxic outcomes.

Drum roll please... **People Leadership** shifts the status quo about leading on its head.

What is People Leadership?

People Leadership is understanding that when people thrive at work, everyone wins.

- People Leaders know that every one of their direct reports is a unique human deserving their unique attention.
- People Leaders are committed to developing the skill of their leadership in its own right.
- People Leaders consciously build team care so that people talk to one another, not about one another.

- People Leaders define and document their internal culture, ensuring that it is healthy and positive for *everyone* who works there.
- People Leaders ask questions, are empathetic for how people experience work, and are empowered and motivated to improve that experience.

The world of leadership gurus is cluttered with stories of individual leaders whose positive characteristics are dramatized and whose negative traits are forgotten, like Steve Jobs and Lee Iacocca.

It is time we stopped viewing People Leadership as a rare instance with a few special people who manage to make millions (billions!) by being on station with a needed or beloved product in a market ripe for it.

Instead, let's adopt the view that good People Leadership is learned.

It is a practice that anyone can develop, although some people may be pre-disposed by personality or upbringing towards high emotional intelligence.

We need leaders who are good for people to make work good.

Because when every employee feels connected, they bring all of their good stuff to work.

My friend Joanne, a research company CEO, said, "Sometimes I feel like the people I work with should have trouble walking through doors. Their heads are so big, and their hearts and bodies are atrophied by comparison." She was so right. In my 30+ years of consulting, training, and coaching, most of my clients have been smart and savvy, often with advanced degrees in technical fields. They're intelligent, educated, and often highly experienced. So why do they call me? Because my work is about relationships between people in the workplace, something they find challenging.

Over the years, I have collected stories that highlight the commonality of people problems at work. A surgery center CEO once told me, somewhat graphically, that he was trained to "cut people," but in his new role as CEO he was being asked to do things for which he was not prepared—to lead, to mentor, to communicate, and to engage partners. The CEO of a small engineering firm told me that his newest engineers were technically excellent but that the firm was losing projects because of their inability to convey empathy and understanding to clients, who felt that they were working with arrogant and "thick" technicians. The number of stories like this—the tech company that flops because its coders are unable to collaborate, the architect whose buildings are beautiful but whose clients don't feel valued, the retail shop owner who can't seem to keep her staff for more than a few months—is astounding. These examples show an atrophy of what I call heart skills— the people in these stories are technically fit for their jobs. Still they lack skills such as self-awareness, social awareness, and emotional intelligence that would enable them to lead, inspire, partner, and create change.

Part of the problem is that the educational approaches of traditional science, medicine, business, engineering, or technology programs don't focus on developing heart skills (empathy, vulnerability, transparency, compassion, courage). When will our academic and professional systems and processes stop growing human beings with big head skills and small, atrophied heart skills? We fail doctors, teachers, engineers, MBAs, architects, managers, and technologists when we don't arm them with a complete set of tools, one that includes activating emotional pathways and emphasizing relationship-building skills. When we fail to teach heart skills, we inadvertently undercut workers' capacity to tackle the big problems they're trained for. Fortunately, this oversight in education keeps me employed, but I would like to see students and employees alike demand and seek out education that goes beyond the technical.

The Four Traits of Heart-Based Leadership

I will use an example of an extremely successful leader to identify those four traits of effective heart-based leadership. I was in the audience of an international conference I'd been attending regularly for more than a decade, where the focus was on bringing together disparate members of one trade. This year there was uneasiness among the attendees, though, because the president of the hosting organization wasn't there. Unknown to most, he was experiencing unforeseen and serious medical issues. He had never missed the conference before, and he was eager to make an appearance. During the conference closing ceremony, the team decided to live-cast him onto the screen of the conference plenary to share a few words. When his face came on the big screen, however, his planned address vanished before he could begin, drowned by the roar of a standing ovation.

He was shocked at this response. As I watched, I could see the emotions on his face: humility, profound gratitude, awe, admiration, fear, and patience. Looking around the audience I saw faces that seemed to say, "We've missed, you and we're so happy to see you. Things were working without you, but your absence has weighed on us, and we want you back."

This audience was a group of people who were willing to follow their leader anywhere. What makes some leaders so compelling to their followers? The incredible leaders I have met, like this one, point to four pillars of heart-based leadership:

- **Emotional Stirring.** The first pillar is one I call *emotional stirring*. As the story above shows, there's an emotional connection between strong leaders and their people. As humans, we're drawn by joy, belief, gratitude, wonder, even fear and recovery. Data and logic help us solve problems and get results, but emotion draws us toward a leader, calls our attention, and makes us listen. We become captivated by our hearts, moved to unexpected expression, and compelled to seek out that emotional stirring again. Inspiring leaders know that emotion isn't something they must get out of the way before getting the work done but is, instead, the core drive that fuels their team.

- **Authentic Vulnerability.** The second trait I call *authentic vulnerability*. The leader on the live-cast showed his followers his fear and gratitude; likewise, the constituents, by way of their applause, expressed their genuine appreciation and admiration of their leader. When leaders show their imperfections, we see them as real and human, and our trust grows. Our tolerance for showmanship, veneer, and ego dancing is very low, and such patterns turn us off from real engagement—leaders who can be vulnerable reveal their courage and their trust in their followers. We'll do anything for leaders who strive for greatness through and with their imperfections.

- **Compelling Belief.** The third trait is having a *compelling belief*. Leaders need a reason to be in the lead. A leader exists for those moments when the way is unclear or the task seems insurmountable. In the case of this leader, he articulated his clear belief in the industry's unity and a deep appreciation of difference in his mission to unify a global trade. His ability to set forward an ambitious, clear, and compelling future for the conference's constituents inspired hope in the participating members. The ability to return to that belief, even when the community was unsure and hesitant, drew followers in and kept them engaged.

- **Harmony Between the Words and the Music.** The fourth and final trait of heart-based leadership is *harmony between the words and the music*. The words are what we say, and the music is the feeling we give others. Dissonance between what we feel and what we hear erodes trust. If leaders say they're hopeful, we want to feel the emotional vibe of hope. If they're anxious and concerned, we want to see that in their faces and understand where that comes from.

In this leader's face, on screen, it was clear that his fear and hope lived simultaneously and captured the dynamic nature of their changing industry and his heart. Humans are skilled at reading subtle, nonverbal communicative cues, and know when someone is faking. This fourth trait requires leaders to understand what they are feeling and to express it in a way that's consistent and aligned with what we feel emanating from them.

With these four traits of heart-based leadership in mind— emotional stirring, authentic vulnerability, compelling belief, and harmony between the words and the music—I'd like to look at some stories that demonstrate the various ways in which different leaders embody them. This section is intended first to give you an intuitive sense of what this type of leadership looks like and then to offer tools you can use to develop heart-based leadership in your Bravespace workplace. In what follows, I will combine my experience with recent research perspectives on profound, heart-based leading.

Leading from the Heart

The CEO of a large medical system demonstrated this quality beautifully during a difficult time for the organization. A violent incident occured in which a patient accosted a staff member with a knife. Police were involved, and although no one was badly hurt, it was traumatic for all. When the team convened after a press conference about the situation had been resolved, the CEO thanked everyone for their courage and perseverance and visibly became emotional about the moments of terror. She simultaneously expressed gratitude, fear, and confidence, which together contributed to her remarks drawing the staff toward her leadership even as she was authentically impacted.

To make work good, leaders must embrace leading with their hearts as well as their heads. In order to do so, leaders need to know themselves, and they need to know themselves well.

Critical Self-Reflection

A grad school professor, Ed Tomey, once told me that the two questions we must ask ourselves as leaders are "Who am I?" and "Who am I with you?" Although these questions are short and simple in form, the answers are neither short nor simple.

I'm 61 years old, and answering these questions is no easier now than it was when I was 22. Sure, I have a better understanding of my flaws, skills, and desires, but I still frequently step in familiar dog doo as I navigate the many personal and professional worlds in which I live and work. For example, although I spoke briefly of socialized gender roles above, I can easily hear the protests of my male audience members—"What do you mean 'white male culture'?" Or the disagreement of people of color, who may have had vastly different experiences navigating the work world. Even as I strive to understand the nuances of what makes a leader effective and to share what I know, I might inadvertently offend or be misunderstood by others. I'm as likely to make mistakes in my interactions with others today, with familiar behavioral gaffs or attitudinal biases, as I was when I started my career.

Part of the impact of these two questions is that the answers to them walk the line between, on the one hand, the pragmatic dogma of business ownership and citizenship, and on the other hand, the spiritual basis of motivation and passion. For example, when I ask myself, "Who am I?" In my professional capacity, my ambition, curiosity, helpfulness, and optimism. But I also encounter my other roles: mom, partner, sister, co-worker, and caregiver. Asking myself, "Who am I with you?" can help to clarify these roles. With my clients I see my gift of optimism, the gift and danger of my high energy, and the vulnerability inherent in depending on others. This second question invites me to consider each of the people in my life constellation, their dreams, their wounds, and their connection to me in ways that make our partnerships purposeful and important rather than random. We interact and we affect each other all the time in every way, whether we mean to or not.

We are human beings, hard-wired for connection, and as a result, we're inextricably tuned in to cause and effect with one another in everything we do. Asking, "Who am I?" in the realm of partnership isn't a complete question when it's not paired with, "Who am I with you?" As a leader, knowing yourself will facilitate an honest expression of your needs, wants, and motivations. It creates the critical pathway for empathy and listening, and it should be the starting point for leaders on the path to making their companies Bravespace workplaces.

Making Mistakes (Yes, Leaders Too)

Being alive means being imperfect. And yet many of us relentlessly work to hide our imperfections as if they're separate from us. Doing so creates cultures of comparison, in which we're frightened and watch others for evidence that we're good enough or close to perfect. Brené Brown (2010)[44] has studied and clarified the dynamics of imperfection and speaks poignantly about mistakes as part of our story: "Owning our story can be hard but not nearly as difficult as spending our lives running from it. Embracing our vulnerabilities is risky but not nearly as dangerous as giving up on love, belonging and joy—the experiences that make us the most vulnerable. Only when we are brave enough to explore the darkness will we discover the infinite power of our light." Paradoxically, when we as leaders show up as real and authentic, people are drawn to us, and when we hustle to appear as if we have it all perfectly together, people keep their distance.

This paradox of being worthy and flawed at the same time is a dynamic I have seen with my clients and my roles as a leader at many levels. I know, for example, that no matter how airtight I make my schedule, I will miss a meeting, pick up my children late, or miss a deadline. I hate it when I make a familiar mistake. But part of what it means for me to lead well is to acknowledge my mistakes. In the situations in which I work, I often see leaders who unwittingly send the message that mistakes are unacceptable, despite our understanding that they're inevitable. What does it take for a leader to make graceful mistakes?

Here are six ways I have seen brave leaders navigate mistakes:

- **Listen to their intuition (really listen) and act on it.** Those times when we ignore what our gut tells us almost always play out badly. Shutting down our natural responses is shutting down our emotional connectedness, our intelligence, and our wisdom born from experience. Why would anyone want to do that?

- **Have compassion and empathy for yourself.** Many of my clients are far more kind and more empathetic to others than they are themselves. They talk to themselves in the privacy of their minds with harshness and even cruelty. Uttering words of care, love, tenderness, forgiveness, and compassion to oneself are ways leaders can walk their talk and recover from missteps.

- **Remember that others are imperfect too.** Nobody else has the secret recipe for perfection, so we can let ourselves off the hook for being imperfect. When did we get the notion that others have all this life stuff figured out and that we didn't get the memo? There is no memo, most of us have lives that are more whirlwind than tidy, and there are no instructions.

- **Notice what trigger you to feel shame, which is vital to a solid People Leadership practice.** Shame is the emotion we experience when we fear we are not enough, that we're not worthy of love and belonging, and when we're triggered into shame, our brains are in survival mode. Usually nothing good comes of it, so it's crucial that we notice, and name shame and not engage in overblown self-flagellation. We can and should stop just short of the cliff edge before our feeling of shame is activated, because when it's triggered we all start hustling to protect ourselves and hustling to feel worthy is never pretty, rarely real, and feels awful.

- **Remember that big risks open big possibilities.** Since I was a little girl, I have pushed myself to extreme pursuits—

acting, mountaineering, whitewater rafting, horseback riding, starting a business. I know the benefits of just jumping in. When I make mistakes, it's often because I'm trying hard, living big, and putting it on the line.

- **Comparing yourself to others is a bad idea.** Always. Comparison is a prevailing curse of Western society in general and women in particular, leading to a whole sequence of bad results. Let's stop comparing ourselves. Comparison is especially dangerous for leaders because employees need to be regarded as unique individuals and for what they uniquely bring to work.

Mistakes have a place in the practice of leadership and at work. Making minor errors along the way allows us to avoid catastrophic mistakes when it counts. Mistakes are essential learning and the learning process, but they're never easy. Making work good requires leaders who make an effort to model tolerance for imperfection, and they see it as part of learning and innovating. By doing so, they invite the people who work for them to take risks and to learn. People are drawn to these leaders because they know they can show up fully as they are and be seen and contribute, even when they're less than perfect.

Leading with Heart is Leading

The stories I've told so far are just some ways that I've seen leaders express the four traits of heart-based leadership. Effective heart-based leaders spend time and effort cultivating relationships. They treat their role as a leader as a practice, not a destination. They craft agreements that honor the unique nature of everyone who works for them, and ensure that people feel seen. They speak what's true, even when it's damn hard, intimidating, emotional, or scary.

Heart-based leaders acknowledge that emotions are important for what we do at work; they're not a private excess that we need to hide. Heart-based leaders lead from the heart (feelings) and from the brain (ideas and knowledge.) They show vulnerability as a means to authentically connect, and are willing to take the first step. Heart-based leaders know that people come to work every day wanting to connect and contribute, and they remember, even when the going gets hard, that their employees are people, not machines.

There are three important myths to debunk when we step into leading with heart:

1. Heart means emotionality. This misconception arises from our worry that our emotion will overtake us and the situation. That is not what we mean when we talk about leaders having heart skills. Emotionality—behaving from intense emotion without intelligent containment—can interrupt communication effectiveness and trust. But by becoming emotionally intelligent, we can utilize our emotions and those of others with the benefit of containing our emotionality.

2. Work and personal well-being are separate. We are the same person and home and work, and whatever societal legacy taught is that these are two separate elements of self was wrong. Period.

3. People issues are soft and can wait. Anyone who has ignored a people dynamic at work and seen it fester, grow,
   and pollute a team and progress knows that the better
   strategy is to dig in as soon as the challenge is named or
   nameable. It is all about when you pay in time, energy, and
   effort. Paying at the front end means investing in prevention and dealing with problems and feelings when they
   are small. Paying later often means coping with magnified
   and multiplied emotions and pain, requiring more profound and harder-to-find repair.

Connection to Yourself

To be a good people leader, you must first and foremost, know
yourself.

Introducing Cassie, a leader who understands the value of a
learning mentality.

"I have a challenging conversation tomorrow with a colleague,"
she said with a big smile. "But I'm so excited about it. I have a
plan. Even if it goes off the rails, it will be productive."

Her enthusiasm was palpable.

Cassie recently graduated from our Leading People Program™
and shared this outcome during our private graduation event.

Her confidence was evident, even in the face of an uncomfortable truth of leadership: no amount of practice and prepara-
tion can prevent hard conversations from being demanding.

But Cassie was okay with that and felt confident jumping in head first.

Not because she's a perfect leader but she's practiced this move frequently.

One of the lies we tell leaders is that they can be good without practice. We imply that the tools and behaviors they need to activate people's talents are inherent in them, and once they are labeled as a "leader," they should just flow out of them.

Why do we expect leaders to be perfect without practice?

Most of the time, people are promoted from individual contributor roles to leadership roles because they are good at their jobs.

- The best engineers are promoted to engineering managers.
- A counselor gets promoted to lead.
- An awesome teacher gets promoted to assistant principal.
- A skilled nurse gets promoted to nurse manager.

And once that promotion is granted, these newly minted People Leaders are expected to lead well, instinctually, and easily.

But there's no correlation between being good at a skilled job and being a good leader.

Most of the time, these people have spent years refining the skills of their profession and have not studied—or even more importantly—haven't practiced leading people.

Usually, they discover they're in deep water quite quickly.

Because these people are naturally hard-working and accustomed to success, they double down.

Perfectionism makes struggling leaders work five times as hard as they need to.

They cover up their challenges by doing more: solving more problems, taking on more tasks, and efforting or hustling to heroically contribute at a "leader-like" level.

Even in the C-Suite, this happens consistently.

I worked with a hospital director who said, "Moe, I'm trained to *cut* people, not lead them." He was a renowned surgeon.

Leaders at every level fake it until they make it, hoping against hope that their expert knowledge and grit will be good enough.

It does not have to be this way.

Leading consists of practical behaviors, mindsets, and skills that can be taught and, more importantly, learned and practiced like any other skill.

It's not some mystical pseudo-science that only the rare few are gifted to comprehend.

We don't teach leadership skills in business school, nursing school, medical school, trade apprenticeships, technical programs, and more. We expect them to know how to lead people and do it well from the start.

A consequence of this is that companies and organizations are left picking up the slack.

Leaders need to embrace the mindset of "practice."

Rather than taking on a hero's mindset that they must know everything, do everything, solve everything, and be good at leading from the get-go, leaders can think of their leadership tenure as one big opportunity to practice.

In other fields, we do not expect the good ones to miraculously show up perfectly.

- Famed Cellist Yo-Yo Ma surely made and still makes lots of squawks and squeaks on his cello when prepping to play at Carnegie Hall.
- Basketball star Michael Jordan, as he has said, has missed more than 9000 shots on the basket in his career and lost 300 games.
- Wilbur and Orville Wright survived many serious crashes before their historic first flight.
- Less than 25% of new businesses make it longer than 10 years.
- The majority of Olympians do not win medals.

So, why do we expect People Leaders not to be learners?

The best place to start is with self-awareness.

Back to Cassie for a minute. When she first connected the dots that her innate personality was oriented towards helpfulness, she developed a keen insight into what was happening in her work relationships.

By over-indexing on taking care of people, she minimized people's struggles and, at worst, overlooked the brave feedback conversations so critical to helping people bring their best to their job. Leaning on her emotional intelligence skills in empathy and relationships, Cassie experimented with more direct, clear, and focused conversations about accountability than ever before.

The result?

She became more skilled at telling the truth about problems and issues without losing compassion.

The result was higher trust, deeper engagement, and better performance from everyone on her team.

And every time she entered a new difficult conversation, her palms still got sweaty. Not all of them went well, she had to repair and recalibrate.

But slowly, over time, Cassie is becoming a better People Leader.

If this continues, she will surely be one of the best by the time she retires.

Leaders are learners.

Learners do it imperfectly and make mistakes.

When People Leaders are authentic, feeling, and imperfect, it facilitates trust in their key partnerships with others. The result is connection, confidence, and collaboration in the teams they lead.

A note about inclusion and belonging.

In my consulting and coaching firms' offerings, we weave diversity, equity, inclusion, and belonging into everything we do. We purposefully do not teach inclusion as an add-on or separate skillset from building teams who care, a conscious and brave culture or, being a leader who is good for people.

Why?

Because mindfully focusing on diversity, equity, and real belongingness are central skills to every leader in every organization.

Period.

To serve the dynamically changing markets of the future, every organizational leader, from Mom and Pop to Mega Corp, will need to be fluent and capable of noticing and naming identity differences, examining and re-designing systems that disproportionately benefit some overall, interrupting oppression, and creating equal opportunity across differences like race, gender, ability, and more. These skills will require grounded confidence, self-awareness, and rigorous courage to build connections in sameness and difference. It is past time that being a People Leader means being skilled at including all people.

Endnotes

43 Gerzema, John, and Michael D'Antonio. 2013. *The Athena Doctrine: How Women (and the Men Who Think Like Them) Will Rule the Future.* San Francisco: Jossey-Bass.

44 Brown, Brené. 2010. *The Gifts of Imperfection: Let Go of Who You Think You're Supposed to Be and Embrace Who You Are.* Center City, MN: Hazelden Publishing.

CHAPTER 10

Clarity

*Indifference towards people and the reality in which they live
is actually the one and only cardinal sin in design.*

—Dieter Rams

The whole event was thoughtfully designed. I had arrived in downtown San Francisco to give a talk and do a book signing at a tech company. From the minute I walked in the door, it felt like home. Someone met me cheerily at the elevator. My greeter gushed with being happy to have me, and whisked me into the cafeteria/auditorium where I would be speaking. My books had been lovingly arranged all around the little elevated stage, where people naturally congregated. There were pens full of ink sprinkled everywhere, and balloons in the corners. Someone put a lavaliere mic on my shirt and quickly adjusted it. I smelled something in the air, and my host said, "Would you like a fresh doughnut?" Their welcome made me feel that I was meant to be there at that moment to talk to those exact people. It felt this way because my hosts carefully designed the event around my needs, audience, my book.

We live in a designed world today. Coe Leta Stafford (2018)[45] the managing director of IDEO U, the educational offshoot of the global design company IDEO, describes human-centered design as the attempt made by organizations to focus on the people they serve. For Stafford, this process "leads to human-centered products, services, and internal processes." What makes design important is this human-centeredness. Design thinking asks how we can design this system, space, or product in a manner that facilitates human well-being and prosperity. In this chapter, I'll talk about what it means to design workplaces that are fit for human life—Bravespace workplaces—by focusing on accountability, time, and the physical structures of an organization. I use the words *space* and *place* differently. Place identifies the many felt components of work—the calendar and scheduling systems, how people communicate, the culture and vibe, the practices, and the energetic atmosphere of the organization. On the other hand, space, refers to the physical location of work—the building, the layout, the wall color, and so on.

Making work good requires us to take design thinking concepts and apply them directly to how work unfolds in four key categories:

- **People:** How are people organized in your organization?
- **Time:** When do your people work? (work hours/flex time)
- **Location:** Where do people work?
- **Impact:** How does your organization impact the communities in which it lives?

How to Organize People: Intentional Structure

It's very rare that a problematic person in a workspace is malicious. More often, problems between people at work stem from how an organization is structured from top to bottom.

Typically, we think of organizational structure as the boxes in an organizational chart, but that merely represents the formal structure of a company, the first layer of the onion. The actual structure lies in how accountability flows through the organization. We use accountability to make and maintain agreements at work. "I need to do this because if I don't, I'll be held accountable by others." This is different from responsibility, which is our internal sense of drive and motivation. "I need to do this, because I want to succeed."

Think of it this way. I like to run and walk. Over the years, my friend Sandy and I have run or walked thousands of miles together, often in the early morning. I do it for fitness, for connection (we talk while we walk), and because I want to. But many times, before the sun comes up, especially when it's raining, I'm tempted to send a quick text to Sandy, "Sorry. Can't make it." What keeps me from doing so is that a) we agreed to meet, b) she's waiting, and c) I know that if I don't show up, she'll tell me that my flakiness left her hanging. I do what I should do because I feel accountable to Sandy. When organizations have "people" problems, those problems are often accountability problems.

Canadian psychoanalyst, social scientist, and management consultant Eliot Jacques (1990) advanced a theory of stratified systems that maintains that when accountability isn't named in the contract between an employer and an employee, both fail. Jacques put it this way: "One of the most widespread illusions in business, namely, [is] that a company's managerial leadership can be significantly improved solely by doing psychotherapeutic work on the personalities and attitudes of its managers." He maintained that "properly structured, hierarchy can release energy and creativity, rationalize productivity, and actually improve morale." In order to do our jobs well—work we're proud of and want to be seen—we need to clearly understand what doing a job well looks like, and to whom we're accountable for doing the work.

In her book, *Dare to Lead*, Brené Brown writes that for courageous leaders, clarity is kindness. Being clear in Bravespace workplaces is kind. Lack of clarity is unkind. And yet the management fad pendulum tends to swing right and left from militaristic hierarchy to chaotic open-team approaches, with very little data to tell us which systems work best for kind clarity.

Most companies organize themselves organically, at least in the beginning. A founder or owner has an idea; they start selling stuff, and then when they need to, they add people. It's a naturally occurring process, and it usually works fine until it doesn't. The tipping point varies, but in my experience, it's often when an organization gets to be around 100 people or $5 million in revenue. Often the wheels come off the bus because the number of people reaches a volume where communication across and within functions becomes unwieldy. The system goes from one in which many people share knowledge and access to one in which not everyone knows what they need to know.

Accountability should be assigned so that every person knows what they need to do and can focus on those things. This is best measured, according to Jacques, by understanding the complexity of a task and the time it takes to complete it. For example, a jewelry design company with 95 employees needs at least a few people to make sure that what needs to happen today is happening (FedEx comes, shipping is received, customers are supported), as well as someone to think ahead to next year ("What product line will launch in what channels?"), and even a few people to consider the multi-year window ("Will we outgrow our space?" "Is manufacturing going to need to be outsourced?" "What if silver costs go up?").

Although the work is daunting, it's not overly complex. Every employee in your organization be able to answer two questions:

- **To whom am I accountable?** In this age of matrixed organizations and collaborative, cross-functional partnerships, we tend to resist single-person accountability. Yet the simplicity and reliability of single-person accountability cannot be overstated. I can work with many people day in and day out, but it's important that I know to whom I must report my successes and failures. If I'm accountable to too many people, I can find a way of skirting my responsibilities by manipulating whom I report to. We need one person at work to whom we're accountable.

- Note that responsibility comes from within us—our internal desire to do something because it matters to us. Accountability comes from between us—we do things we have committed to doing because we are accountable to another. Noticing and naming the difference allows us to make sure accountabilities are clear even when someone is highly personally responsible.

- **What does "doing a job well" look like?** We can track qualitative and quantitative specifics to know if we are doing a job well. Nonetheless, despite nearly 80 years of HR-driven rating and ranking approaches to performance management, we have no evidence that employee rating and ranking systems improves people's performance. According to professors Peter Cappelli and Anna Tavis (2016)[46]:

  o One *Washington Post* business writer called annual performance ratings a "rite of corporate kabuki" that restricts creativity, generates mountains of paperwork, and serves no real purpose. Others have described annual reviews as a last-century practice and blamed them for lack of collaboration and innovation. Employers are also finally acknowledging that supervisors and subordinates despise the appraisal process—a perennial problem that feels more urgent now that the labor market is picking up and concerns about retention have returned.

What are the implications for Bravespace workplaces? Hopefully, the result is more frequent, compassionate, honest, and rigorous person-to-person conversations about how things are going than we have had in the past. People learn in different ways on the job, and the career paths they'll take in the workplaces of tomorrow are hard to predict. In the future, there will be jobs that we can't imagine today, and it's predicted that people will have twelve to fifteen careers in a lifetime, so performance and development depend on personal, meaningful conversations between managers and employees about where they're going.

These conversations will facilitate what Deloitte (Buckley and Bachman 2017)[47] describes as a "series of developmental experiences, each offering a person the opportunity to acquire new skills, perspectives, and judgment." Careers in this century may follow an upward arc, with progression and promotion at various times, but they'll look nothing like the simple stair-step path of generations ago.

We teach a simple process called The Monthly Meet-Up that guides the People Leader and the Employee through a dialogue-based approach that explores how things are truly going, rather than the endless list of tasks we tend to talk about with ease.

The Monthly Meet-Up

PERFORMANCE ACHIEVEMENT
MONTHLY MEET-UP TEMPLATE (3-C'S)

	EMPLOYEE	LEADER
CELEBRATE	1. Share something you are proud of this month? (i.e. proactive action you took, goal you reached, important conversation you had, team success, etc.) 2. What feels like it is going well here? What is working? 3. How are you doing with personal well being and work/life integration?	**Listen for and share:** - Appreciations to reinforce work (focus on values) - Specific observations and wins that the employee may not have mentioned (your "keep doing more of this" observations!) **Questions:** 1. What has enlivened you and given you positive energy? 2. What do you feel good about having accomplished or learned? 3. How are you doing with personal well being and work/life integration?
COLLABORATE	1. What support, reinforcement, education, or help do you need to succeed next month? 2. What ideas do you have for focus next month? Where will you put your energy? 3. What will a great month look like next time? *This is the part where you may receive critical or improvement related feedback. Remember, the more you know about your impact the more effective you will be. Listen and be open, even when it is hard. This is also the section where you can share feedback with your Manager--it is important to them to know their impact, too!*	**Listen for and share** - Specific feedback on refinement or improvement opportunities - Validate if their focus looks spot-on or off-base **Questions** 1. How do you feel about what coming up this month? 2. Where are you feeling over or underwhelmed? 3. Are you clear on priorities? 4. What support or help can I provide? 5. What I am hoping to see and/or notice? (focus for improvement) 6. What feedback do you have for me? (I really want to know your candid feedback on how I am doing upside and downside!) 7. How is progress on your goals? *This is is the part where, you will share your critical or improvement feedback Clear is kind, unclear is unkind. Remember to share about the impact someone is having by using direct but compassionate language*
CONFIRM	1. What do I need from my leader or company? 2. What will I be focusing on this month at work? 3. What will I start/stop/continue? 4. What support do I need?	**"Thank you so much for checking in"** **"Anything else you need from me/from anyone else here?"** **"Keep up your awesome work!"**

Consider When We Work

A potent currency in today's workplaces is the ability to flex work hours. The global pandemic sent most workers home for a timeframe that stretched from days to years, leaving most organizations scrambling to figure out the new work rules when people do not occupy the same space or hours.

Although most businesses are open from 9 a.m. to 5 p.m., we all have a time that's best for us to work and get things done. For me, it's hours of 4 a.m. and 7 a.m. My brain is most alert then, and I feel capable of anything. On the other hand, mid-afternoon, I generally start to drag. But no matter when we may be most productive, we live in a world of schedules imposed on us by others—shops, schools, children, flights, and so on.

One of the most significant demands on people's work schedules is taking care of children and parents. Schedule conflicts at work tend to increase when children are involved, and these conflicts can vary with their ages and individual needs. Greater family demands—more children or adult dependents at home—frequently create a need for more flexible or less-demanding work conditions. Job requirements that an employee once enjoyed or tolerated, such as weekend hours or extensive travel, can suddenly create significant stress. Traditionally women have carried the burden of juggling work with family. While that's still true to a great extent, men are increasingly taking on more responsibility at home instead of sacrificing their personal lives to their jobs' demands.

Flexible schedules work well for many of us because they enable us to clearly distinguish between time at work and time in other roles. These are my work hours, and these are my life hours. Other individuals prefer integrating work and family roles throughout the day, trading text messages with our children from the office or monitoring emails at home and on vacation rather than returning to work to find hundreds of email messages waiting to be dealt with.

Another time factor for many individuals is how long it takes to commute to work. As people become busier, time becomes increasingly valuable, and every hour counts. One study conducted by Canada's University of Waterloo (Hilbrecht et al. 2014)[48] concluded that people with the longest commutes have the lowest overall satisfaction with life. The authors report that commute lengths are linked to time pressure. People who spend the most time on the road experience higher stress levels of stress because they constantly feel hurried. Many spend much of their time on the road worrying about all the activities they're missing.

As workers demand more flexibility, work is structured more broadly. We see less of the "enterprise shift" (9 a.m. to 5 p.m.) as more and more employees move to adjunct or "gig" situations, often primarily to meet their lifestyle needs. In the United States, more than 40% of workers are now employed in alternative work arrangements, such as contingent, part-time, or gig work, and this percentage is steadily rising, increasing by 36% in just the past five years (Agarwal et al. 2018)[49.] Some workers today aren't satisfied with traditional nine-to-five work hours; they prefer to schedule their work around hobbies, caregiving, and other aspects of their lifestyles. These changes place new demands on employers.

The presiding win I am seeing in the post-COVID era is clarity with adaptability. Employees typically, but not always, prefer flexible work hours. Employers, often want employees to be clearly working at certain times. It works best when everyone is crystal clear on when they are to be working and when not.

But for salaried positions, certain types of work are often done in non-traditional hours to meet life integration needs (i.e., taking a call from a soccer game, or working a Saturday when there are no likely interruptions). In these cases, the clarity that matters is not so much when the work is done but what good looks like.

Defining "good" in terms of employee output means agreeing to QQTR:

- Quality: What is the expected qualitative standard for this work?
- Quantity: How many or how much is done to be considered sufficient?
- Time: When is the work due or to be done by?
- Resources: What resources are available for completing this task or deliverable?

Defining QQTR helps to make accountability transparent between employees and people leaders and can save needless conversations about work hours.

While the stress of competing obligations is increasing, our willingness to make personal sacrifices for work is decreasing. As workplaces realize this, norms, expectations, and practices are changing. When these conflicting demands compete for our finite time and emotional energy, our work and other relationships and responsibilities also suffer. In a study conducted by Barry Posner and Jim Kouzes (2010)[50,] 50% of managers agreed with the statement, "Anxiety about my job frequently spills over into my home and personal life." In a study by researchers Danielle Talbot and Jon Billsberry (2010)[51,] 68% of the participants mentioned that their families, other social networks and connections, or obligations to their communities affected their fit at work. Changing societal norms, such as the influx of women into the workforce, the increased prevalence of dual-earner couples, movement away from traditional gender-based roles, and technology that blurs the line between work and personal time, all contribute to the challenge. When you add factors such as the tremendous growth in single parents and employees taking care of aging relatives, lifestyle challenges affect all of us.

Leaders of Bravespace workplaces need to figure out how people's work times affect the business. For some companies, such as those that deal with customers, academic institutions, and medical facilities, the need to be open during specific hours requires workers to be at particular locations at specific times.

But for many others, work can be done anytime. And—in fact, the work will likely be better if work times and places can flex to fit employees' natural rhythms, needs, and habits.

Workplace data due to COVID-19 has made this more visible than ever.

The Myth of Work-Life Balance

Work-life balance is regarded as a harmonious unity between when and how one works and when and how one lives. This balance is often talked about in terms of a schedule. Work-life balance, some say, looks like this:

7:00 a.m.: I wake up naturally with the sunlight, fully rested after nine hours of sleep (yeah, I go to bed at 10:00).

7:15 a.m.: I read my gratitude journal over a fresh-pressed, organic French roast.

7:45 a.m.: I go to the gym, where I do the workout that fits perfectly into the yearlong training scheme that was last year's New Year's resolution.

8:45 a.m.: I shower, dress, and enjoy my bike commute (the reason I moved).

9:00 a.m.: At work, I attend a few meetings. They are joyful, and I feel grateful to work with people who feel like friends. I also sink into some focused creative production.

12:00 p.m.: I eat the nutritional (and delicious) lunch I prepared last night.

5:10 p.m.: I bike home, taking the long way to enjoy the setting sun.

6:00 p.m.: I eat a satisfying dinner with my partner, read my children bedtime stories, and write in my gratitude journal.

8:00 p.m.: My partner and I have an open, easy, rewarding conversation (something we practice a lot), make love, and drift off to sleep right on time.

Ah, the balanced day—time for work, play, connection, and self-care.

Of course, I've never experienced a day like this one. My days, and I suspect many of yours, consist of periods of intensity and chaos, energizing hard conversations, just-in-time reports rushed to the post office, meetings prepped for and noted, an occasional collapse into a Netflix binge, sometimes a yoga class or a delightful novel. Regardless of what my days look like on a calendar, very little about my life *feels* balanced as it is happening. The felt quality of my days is much more dynamic—at times, I'm transfixed and fully occupied in what I do; at other times my mind wanders and I wish I were elsewhere. I'm constantly weighing tradeoffs, and compromises, punctuated by delight, brilliance, mess, and sweat. I often feel guilty that my life doesn't match the images I have of a perfectly balanced life. I feel deeply inadequate when I have to reschedule an obligation or adjust my expectations, admitting to myself that I can't do it all. These feelings billow into an anxious fear that I've become a workaholic, someone who can't stop obsessing about work.

At other moments, though, I recognize that work-life balance doesn't have to match how I feel. In these moments, I have the clarity and courage to say to the world, "Look! It's working! This dance, the wildly out-of-balance, CEO-mom-sister-wife-friend-former-athlete-wanna-be-creative-writer dance, is moving to the music! Somehow, my business is working, I have people who love me, and what I do is making a difference somewhere." These moments of gratitude, amid the felt chaos of my life, feel like a third option between perfect balance and workaholism.

I have a few role models who seem to live the same way. Michelangelo worked for days on end while painting a fresco that he loved. My architect father was always sketching in his book—on vacation, in the kitchen, at dinner. When we love what we do, it becomes us, fully, completely, and powerfully. When the work is worth doing, we don't mind doing it. We're lucky to have those moments when the clock stops, and we lose awareness that this is "work." Employers should bottle up those employee moments as an asset.

Bravespace workspaces recognize that work has a natural place in our lives. It expands and contracts according to the needs of the employer and the employee, and it's important to monitor the impact of the ratio of work and life on the health of the individual and the organization. If we want to work hard sometimes, we should! No guilt, no shame. It feels good, matters to the world, and gets things done. And we should remember, while we work, that rest and play enable us to grow.

Consider Where We Work (Remote, Home, and Space)

McKinsey estimates that 62% of working Americans worked at home during COVID-19 lockdown, and 80% or those workers reported enjoying working from home, with 68% saying that they felt more or as productive at home as they did at work.

Offices are still sitting empty or being re-purposed. The war amongst the big-tech companies to build the most modernistic and comfortable campus has simmered down, with many people in tech now working remotely or impacted by downsizing.

Because many organizations are doing hybrid work, the ambience of work location and its suitability to support the needs of people when they do come together is becoming increasingly important, motivating some companies to do away with traditional cubicles and glass-partitioned offices.

We need to feel safe and equipped for success in our workplaces—out of the elements, with the tools we need to do our job, and with adequate light, air, and temperature control. Beyond that, the physical requirements for workspaces vary greatly, and individual tastes for comfort, beauty, design, and privacy are highly subjective.

Making Work Good in terms of physical space today approaches physical space and ergonomics with a thoughtful mindset about what their employees want and need. What kinds of human interactions are required to get work done? Do workers interact with customers? Should leaders be visible and accessible? Is there a need for privacy?

Since office design, furniture, and ambiance are often costly, the Bravespace workplaces I have seen have had their workplaces consciously designed to enhance and support the work that needs to be done and enable people to thrive. For example, one of my clients had a delightful workspace consisting of simple modular offices attached to a barn. The space was special because it was easy and comfortable for staff to move between the barn and the offices during their workday. The facility was a therapeutic riding program, and the indoor barn, where most of the staff spent most of their time and where services were delivered, was the most critical aspect of a healthy and vibrant workspace. But the team also needed desks, computers, and phones, which were kept in the modular offices, which, while clean and quiet, were far from fancy.

Many workplaces don't need (or want) employees to come to work at their location. Organizations can simultaneously reduce overhead and offer remote work as a benefit to employees. The primary drawback for remote workers is the loss of interaction with colleagues and the chance to synergistically connect with other people for ideas and dialogue. Bravespace workplace leaders design ways for remote workers to occasionally meet and connect with other people at work as a supplement to time on the phone and video conferencing.

What rings critical for hybrid or full remote work situations is that the times when people gather be well-designed. I have seen clients require people to return to the office only to find that everyone is in their own cubicle or private space taking video conference calls, which misses the evocative nature of the synergies of being able to be together for connection at specific times.

The differences between connecting physically and via phone/ video are nuanced but important. We can see less of one another on video and may miss physical messages of body language that give context. Most importantly, though, when we're not in the same physical space, we cannot "feel" each other the same way in terms of our limbic brain (which processes emotion) responses. We can come close, but the pheromone and hormonal communication channels are limited when we are not together in the same space. This is why leaders must consider occasional face-to-face time with their teams, even when working remotely.

Endnotes

45 Stafford, Coe Leta. 2018. "What Is Design Thinking?" IDEO U. https://www.ideou.com/blogs/inspiration/what-is-design-thinking.

46 Cappelli, Peter, and Anna Tavis. 2016. "The Performance Management Revolution." *Harvard Business Review* (October). https://hbr.org/2016/10/the-performance-management-revolution.

47 Buckley, Patricia, and Daniel Bachman. 2017. "Meet the U.S. Workforce of the Future: Older, More Diverse, and More Educated." *Deloitte Review* (July 31). https://www2.deloitte.com/insights/us/en/deloitte-review/issue-21/meet-the-us-workforce-of-the-future.html.

48 Hilbrecht, Margo, Bryan Smale, and Steven E. Mock. 2014. "Highway to Health? Commute Time and Well-Being among Canadian Adults." *World Leisure Journal* 56 (2): 151–63. https://doi.org/10.1 080/16078055.2014.903723.

49 Agarwal, Dimple, Josh Bersin, Gaurav Lahiri, Jeff Schwartz, and Erica Volini. 2018. *Deloitte Insights: The Rise of the Social Enterprise.* https://www2.deloitte.com/content/dam/insights/us/articles/ HCTrends2018/2018-HCtrends_Rise-of-the-social-enterprise.pdf.

50 Posner, Barry, and Jim Kouzes. 2010. *The Truth About Leadership: The No-Fads, Heart-of-the-Matter Facts You Need to Know.* San Francisco: Jossey-Bass.

51 Talbot, Danielle, and Jon Billsberry. 2007. "Employee Fit and Misfit: Two Ends of the Same Spectrum?" 1st Global e-Conference on Fit, The Open University.

CHAPTER 11

Compassion

I've been watching Ted Lasso—and holy cow is there some awesome leadership wisdom in this show.

I want to talk about a scene that shows the limits of measuring your employees' success on metrics alone.

If you've never seen Ted Lasso, let me quickly set the scene. The character Ted Lasso is an eccentric manager of a premier football (soccer) team. Part of Ted's job as the manager is to track the health of his athletes. No doubt he times their runs weighs them and measures their strength. Surely, Ted has a whole sub-team of staff who carefully film and analyze every game the team plays. But one day, one of their star players has a leg injury that keeps him from playing.

Suddenly, it doesn't matter how fast he can run or how much he can lift. All that matters is finding a way to help him heal as effectively as possible. In other words, Ted Lasso's standard metrics can't account for outlying issues like injuries.

The metrics we use for measuring our success don't matter when we're broken.

In the face of dramatic change, the metrics have to change.

"How much did you lift today?" becomes "How's your leg doing today?"

To get his star player back on the team, Ted Lasso had to throw out all of the careful metrics and data and shift to supporting and measuring his player's recovery.

What does this mean at your job?

I can nearly guarantee someone on your team is walking around with a broken leg—if only metaphorically. Times are tough right now.

Mental health in the workplace has been down since the pandemic hit the world, and it hasn't rebounded.

Stress levels are through the roof—especially for People Leaders.

Despite the pressures and the increasing cracks and fissures we're seeing in worker health, not many businesses are pivoting to measure different things.

Have your metrics changed?

Do you tune into and track your employee engagement? How about their mental health?

Leaders everywhere need to take responsibility for their employees' well-being.

Care for your employees' emotional health.

The default check-in question at work is "How are things?"

And the default answer?

Come on... I know you know it.

"Fine."

"Good."

"Okay."

Asking people, "how are things?" or "how are you?" isn't adequate for assessing well-being.

It is best if you get specific—book one-on-ones to check in with your people.

Ask them how they're feeling in their role.

Use specific, open-ended questions like these—heck, you can even steal this for your next one-on-one if you want:

- What was the highlight of your week?
- Where have you failed in the past week?
- What's on your mind?

- What are the three most important things you want to get done by our next meeting?
- What about this conversation was most and least helpful?

Only when we get specific will we find antidotes to our pain.

One helpful tool in framing these conversations around your employees' needs is the seven needs we have of work that we covered in Chapter 2.

You can put any of those needs in the formula below to get insightful questions.

"What makes you feel _____?"

Send it to your employees before your one-on-ones. Read through yourself and ask about what you need.

Try journaling for 10 minutes, using the specific and nuanced words from the worksheet.

Talking About Mental Health

As I walked into the office (okay, I'm lying, it was a Zoom call), someone asked a very familiar question: "How're things?"

I replied curtly, "Good! Good," and moved right along.

When did you last tell someone at work how you're feeling?

It can be super refreshing to let people know what's happening in your life.

An honest check-in with your colleagues can support everyone's mental health at work.

According to Dr. Vivek Murthy, US Surgeon General, "At any moment, about one out of every two Americans is experiencing[52] measurable levels of loneliness[53]. This includes introverts and extroverts, rich and poor, and younger and older Americans. Sometimes loneliness is set off by the loss of a loved one or a job, a move to a new city, or health or financial difficulties—or a once-in-a-century pandemic."

Loneliness and isolation hurt individuals and communities. They are associated with poor health outcomes, decreased work productivity, decreased school performance, and lower civic engagement. It's beyond time we stopped stigmatizing loneliness and mental health, especially at work, and embraced it as simply part of our health.

So, it isn't our things or even our people that give us the most fulfillment. It's what we do with them.

It's not the pile of burning logs; it's the energy at the late-night bonfire. It's not the tent under the stars; it's the sense of adventure and camaraderie we'll carry to the grave. It's the richness of our experiences that matter.

We're in an epidemic of loneliness, and the solution isn't technology. The good news is that we're born to make connections. The problem is that we live in a world that drives us apart. And while the burden of loneliness isn't equal, the path toward a better future is clear.

Every interaction with another is an opportunity to build lasting and meaningful connections—at work or home. It's time to get darn good at it.

More than three out of every five Americans say they're lonely. Even more report feeling left out, misunderstood, or lacking companionship[54].

It's not just the pain of a lonely heart we're dealing with here. Insurance companies—ever tenacious researchers—have quantified and qualified the adverse health effects of long-term loneliness.

Loneliness is an actual disease. And while it's commonly categorized as a mental health problem, more and more research is documenting the harmful physical effects of loneliness.

It is more dangerous than smoking and precipitates suicidal ideation, Alzheimer's disease, and other dementia disorders, not to mention the additional strain on the immune and endocrine systems. All told loneliness is a primary latent cause of many hospitalizations.

Loneliness at work also wreaks havoc on productivity, dramatically increases churn (a massive cost to employers), and contributes to workers feeling burnt out, disengaged, and miserable.

In a culture that often sends its elders away, it might be easy to tell ourselves that the old are the lonely ones. But this just isn't true. Both the severity and prevalence of loneliness are highest in the youngest generation.

Loneliness can't be solved by tech.

The internet was born to connect academic and military re-searchers. Since its inception, the internet has been intended to make connections. But we're starting to see its limits almost two decades since some clever technical minds took digital connection mainstream (I'm looking at you, Zuck).

We know from multiple studies that heavy social media users are lonelier than light users. The very mechanisms the tech industry wants us to use to build connections are, at best, very ineffective and, at worst, prey upon our attention to sell advertising.

The realities of social media and the harm it can cause is start-ing to get depressing. But the good news is that humans are hard-wired for connection. A recent study[55] has shown that vagal tone—a measure of the strength of the neurons that link our brains with our heart—develops more in participants who practiced empathy and connection with others. Vagal tone is directly related to heart-rate variability, a vital indicator of overall health.

Practice love and your body gets healthier. Our brains need it, our bodies need it, and our spirits need it. And we're good at it.

It's just that when we aren't building healthy, meaningful con-nections with people throughout our lives, we suffer and soci-ety is impacted.

Historically, children have not been given practical but challenging relationship-building skills like accountability, vulnerability, or boundary setting in school.

By the time children leave high school, they are equipped with massive stores of knowledge—calculus, biology, medieval history—but are increasingly under-equipped to build strong, resilient bonds in their communities. Thankfully in recent years, the uptick in focus on SEL (Social and Emotion Learning) in schools coming out of the global pandemic is introducing these skills to children when they are young.

And yet, despite our emphasis on social skills recently, at present, the burden of loneliness isn't spread equally.

Men are 1.7 times more likely to be lonely, 3.7 times more likely to commit suicide, and 39 times more likely to commit mass gun murder. I became interested in these differences and addressed them in my 2019 TEDx talk, Loving Men: Women's Role in Healthy Masculinity. What I learned profoundly concerns me.

Yes, the gender category we call "man" is in a dangerous state. It has to do with loneliness and lack of community[56].

Men can have a hard time connecting authentically with other men.

In the mold of the traditional gender role, women are taught to tend to social well-being. From a young age, they are encouraged to be tender, express their feelings, and pay attention to what others are doing and feeling. As a result, women carry an unequal burden of domestic life. In intense family conversations, they serve as the bringers for social gatherings and the keepers of the peace.

Meanwhile, men are taught to push through pain, whether in sports or trauma—to stifle their tears. Tears, it turns out, are a wonderful data point for gauging emotional states.

As children, young boys often exhibit incredible sensitivity to social dynamics and care deeply for their peers. By teenagerhood, the identical boys become indifferent to each other's pain.

It's time to teach men to open their hearts wide and retrain their vagal nerves.

But the path is clear.

Our ingrained habits change us. As neuroscientists repeat, neurons that fire together wire together. In other words, we are doomed to repeat the things we repeatedly do.

Do you open your phone when you feel stressed? Do it enough, and the brain will fill in the gap: stress means you will unlock your phone.

Every interaction is an opportunity to build lasting and meaningful connections.

So, you've never been taught how to forge connections or harness strong accountability. That's okay. Old dogs *can* learn new tricks—given the complicated physiology of connection, our bodies know what to do. All we need to do is practice.

Our state of mind and hearts affect us all deeply.

What's more, workplaces where people feel they can talk about their mental health openly—and are given time and space to care for their mental health—are more humane and outperform toxic, unhealthy workplaces.

Here are eight tips to help you talk about mental health at work:

1. **Ask people how they're doing.** Take a minute to look them in the eye. With curiosity, ask them how things are going. If things are tough in your work environment, you can say, "I know things are tough right now. I want to know how you're doing."

2. **Tell others how you're doing.** Stop hiding in the bathroom or staring numbly at the Zoom call. Own it. "I'm struggling to stay focused today. I'm numb and tuning out." When you own your feelings, you normalize vulnerability and authenticity. When you say, "Yeah, today's been hard for me," you give others permission to do the same.

3. **Normalize words** like anxious, lonely, worried, depression, addiction, self-harm, and mental health.

4. **Model self-compassion.** You're a person too. Kristin Neff offers valuable tools in her interview with Shankar Vedantam on his Hidden Brain Podcast—give it a listen.

You can find many more resources on self-compassion on Neff's website www.self-compassion.org.

5. **Stop problem-solving for each other.** Practice listening with your heart, not your head.

6. **Acknowledge that how you feel affects your capacity to do your best work.** When you're feeling good, give it your all. When you're not, own it.

7. **If you're a leader, grant leaves for mental health days**, counseling appointments, and other needed health care just like you would a medical issues. Do so without incredulity, questions, or raised eyebrows.

8. **Create structures and resources to help employees cope**[57]. Such as employee assistance programs, on-site counseling appointments, mental health first aid, upskilling managers for dealing with mental health.

Every People Leader's Most Important Tool.

Empathy.

But people never believe me when I tell them that. They look at me, surprised. Maybe even incredulous.

Once we start talking about it, the truth comes out. Most people haven't even thought of empathy as a People Leadership tool. Or they've been told they suck at it, so they stopped trying to get good at it.

Theresa Wiseman, a nursing scholar, describes empathy as having four parts:

1. Perspective taking – believing that someone's perspective is true and real for them.

2. Staying out of judgment – refusing to have an opinion about the rightness or wrongness of someone's perspective or feelings.

3. Recognizing emotion – noticing what they might be feeling about the situation.

4. Communicating emotion – the ability to let yourself feel a little bit of what they feel—emotions are familiar to us all, so even if we haven't been in that situation, we know the emotion.

When we are good at empathy, the other person feels seen, believed, and valued.

When we blow it with empathy, they feel unseen, discounted, defensive, and unvalued.

The most common mistake we make with empathy is to add a fifth step that offers advice. Jumping in with answers conveys the underlying message of "You can't handle this; you need me to take care of it for you."

Most of us want to be able to solve our problems, and if we can't, we can ask for help. Let people ask you or ask them if they want some help.

If not, your empathy is enough and, in fact, everything.

Empathy costs nothing but our attention and a willingness to hold space.

Endnotes

52   https://newsroom.thecignagroup.com/loneliness-epidemic-persists-post-pandemic-look

53   https://pubmed.ncbi.nlm.nih.gov/31203639/

54   https://newsroom.thecignagroup.com/loneliness-in-america

55   https://lindagraham-mft.net/neurobiology-social-connection/

56   https://www.economist.com/united-states/2022/01/01/why-men-are-lonelier-in-america-than-elsewhere; https://www.psychologytoday.com/us/blog/life-smarts/202102/the-pandemic-male-loneliness; https://remakingmanhood.medium.com/the-terrible-price-of-our-epidemic-of-male-loneliness-5be6463fd0e0

57   https://hbr.org/2018/11/we-need-to-talk-more-about-mental-health-at-work

CHAPTER 12

Actions for People Leadership

For Leaders or Business Owners

Connection

- Learn about emotions: yours and theirs.
- Develop a courage practice by being vulnerable and going first.
- Walk your talk (including your imperfections and mistakes).
- Give time for real connection at work.
- Ask yourself, "Who am I?" "Who am I with you?"
- Match your words to your music (feelings).
- Get feedback from your people with surveys, pulse checks, or conversations about how you're doing.
- Write a User Manual about how you roll, what you value, what you need to thrive, and more.
- Invest in becoming skilled and self-aware of your cultural competence in of diversity, equity, inclusion, and belonging.
- Hold accountability for leaders to be good for people (all people.)

Clarity
- Think about the accountability flow as you solidify your structure and put people in roles accordingly.
- Remember how far ahead your workers have to think and how complex that thinking needs to be impacts the healthy flow of expectations between managers and employees.
- Thoughtfully decide when people work, and ensure that you understand and can explain the context of those decisions to your workers.
- Make your space (office, shop, etc.) match your culture.
- Have frequent, honest, and wholehearted conversations about what "doing a job well" looks like and how things are going. Banish ratings and rankings.
- Examine and interrupt policies and legacy systems that disrupt equity and disproportionately benefit some over others.
- Be an ally to the under-represented.

Compassion
- Elevate the heart (feelings) and practice empathy.
- Work on being self-compassionate.
- Get good at humble inquiry, asking questions that are ambiguous and personal and that you do not already know the answer to.
- Listen to understand.
- Educate yourself about the lived experience of people different than you and believe them when they tell you their stories.

For Employees

Connection
- Talk to your people leader about how connected you feel to them (or not).
- Learn about difficult conversations and have them more often.
- Think of feelings as a data source and share them with an open heart.
- Be curious about your identity and the identities of your colleagues.
- Be in allyship with people who are different than you.

Clarity
- Make sure that you understand the needs and expectations of the company you join when it comes to work hours, work location, and flexibility, and make sure that these requirements fit into your life.
- Ask the hard questions when you feel your company is out of sync with what they said when you started working for them.
- Participate in open, two-way performance conversations to learn and ensure that you're meeting expectations.
- Try to associate with other people at work, even if you're working remotely, to build a real connection with them.
- Be a community citizen by caring for the workplace you inhabit as if it's your own.

Compassion

- Be generous—most of us are doing the best we can.
- Get good at empathy.
- Educate yourself about people who have different identities than you.

For HR or People Experience (if they exist in your company)

Connection

- Create tools for regular brave and connecting performance conversations for people leaders.
- Define programs for leader learning, including the practice of emotional intelligence and difficult conversations.
- Give leaders feedback on their relationships.
- Hold senior leaders responsible for being brave.
- Invest in education and support for talking about difference and allyship.
- Create spaces where people can talk freely about inclusion.

Clarity

- Move away from ratings and rankings (they don't work); focus on frequent conversations.
- Assess the company's structure regularly to ensure that accountability flow makes sense and is working for everyone.
- Banish rating and ranking systems. Find a human-friendly way for employees and managers to discuss what "doing a job well" looks like and how the work is going.
- Consider peer-to-peer feedback mechanisms. We care a great deal about what our colleagues think.

- Challenge leaders to invest in leadership learning and team development instead of overspending on surface perks.
- Examine policies and practices at work that disproportionately benefit some people over others and change them.
- Offer training and workshops that invite learning about differences and belongingness and how to create it at work.

Compassion

- Teach how values manifest themselves behaviorally at work.
- Offer training and workshops on empathy and self-compassion.
- Build systems of accountability that assume a growth mindset.
- Build systems and policies that are rooted in compassion.

Remote Employees—How to Stay Connected

Every time I travel, I meet people who do the most amazing things in a home office, occasionally traveling to be with clients or colleagues in person. The age of interconnectedness leaves us wondering how best to manage the unique dynamics of remote workers. Distances vary from a few blocks to a few continents.

Companies large and small leverage technology to assist in remote partnerships. They use sophisticated video and teleconferencing features to facilitate employees' ability to see and hear each other in real time. Frequent travel, email, and online communication allow people to share information, outputs, decision-making, and tactical progress.

But even with all these aids that allow people to work together across distances and time zones, people are often frustrated because they don't feel connected. What do they mean by this? If their work outputs are clearly defined and progress is easily traceable, why do people not feel connected with one another? And, more importantly, how can this problem be remedied?

People miss the authentic, emotional connection that's so easy to establish when they're face-to-face with one another, having informal interactions, and passing in the hall. Daniel Goleman, Richard Boyatzis, and others use the term *resonance* to indicate a dimension of emotional intelligence relating to the ability to become attuned to one another, often on an unconscious, subliminal level.

Suggestions for Remove Working Situations

- Preserve and prioritize time with remote workers for pure connection, not just project status, updates, and details.
- Ask questions of one another, such as:
  - "What's new with you?"
  - "What success are you proud of this month?"
  - "What's getting in your way of success these days?"
  - "How are you feeling about our interactions and the clarity of our roles?"
  - "What are you looking forward to next?"
  - "How's your family?"

- Take a portion of planned video or phone meetings to offer non-tactical, personal connection.
- Use applications such as Zoom, Skype, and Google Hangouts as an alternative to phone calls and computer multi-tasking to establish a visual connection.
- Look at people and do not multi-task on video calls.

Remember that establishing an emotional connection takes intention more than it takes time. Five or ten minutes of mutual investment in partnership can bridge the gap far more efficiently than reams of emails and project updates.

PART IV

Build a Conscious, Brave Culture

CHAPTER 13

Plant

Wake up. True change demands action, not passive acceptance.
There is deep beauty in being strong, in being fearless.
There are no mountains high enough. Be awake. Be mindful.
Create the life you want to live and live that life, not the ones
other people want you to conform to. Be the change. With each
action, each thought, each word, each intention.

—Angela Davis

I was in Maine, visiting a lifelong friend and her daughter. My friend likes to take naps. During one of them, I took her daughter and mine to a local thrift store, left them there, and took myself out on an ice cream date. Ice cream store culture is familiar—I grew up eating and working in one on Cape Cod (the infamous Four Seas Ice Cream). The shop I found on this recent day took me right back to that summer job.

It was cool inside. On the walls hung family portraits, and it smelled like sweet, fresh, homemade ice cream. Even more than those material similarities, I noticed was the business's culture. The layout was confusing, so when I entered, I stood around, unsure if they waited on the tables or if I ought to order from the register. While I was hovering, the owner caught my eye and asked, "Would you like to enjoy a treat here or take one with you?" He was inviting, efficient, and kind. I told him two scoops of the double chocolate for here would delight me. The chocolate was on the other side of the store, so he asked an employee to get it. She seemed willing and happy and double-checked my order politely. I was caught by the ease and efficiency of these two. I felt the carefree bliss of a child out of school for the summer, spending her precious pennies on an ice cream cone. As I sat and enjoyed my cone, I continued to watch this little team. It was clear that the way they did things carried the energetic ease that I felt.

Maybe you've had a customer experience like this one—you enter a store and can immediately feel something about it. Sometimes those experiences are negative; maybe a salesperson is too pushy or a customer service agent a bit impatient, or perhaps those experiences are positive, like the one I described. We call this feeling at work "culture."

Organizational culture is like the air we breathe. We don't always feel its presence until it changes. It encompasses how things are done at an organization, and it impacts the feeling of a workspace, for customers and employees, in a big way, for two key reasons. First, organizational culture determines an organization's ability to sustain its health over time via performance and results, and second, it shows employees and customers what the experience of working with that organization is like, whether the employees bring their best to their work. Culture is easy to break but hard to fix.

What is Culture?

Culture is often defined simply as "the way we do things here," and it profoundly impacts how we thrive at work. Jean described it this way: 45.

"I couldn't understand why the culture didn't work well for me at my first job. On the surface, it seemed ideal. But over time, it became clear that the way people acted with each other reflected beliefs and values that were inconsistent with what mattered to me. It came to a head when I noticed a pattern of senior leaders regularly presenting new ideas from their teams as their own. It just didn't sit well with me because it felt that the people doing the work were invisible."

People around the world have become very curious about culture and its role in organizations. With unemployment rates continuing to decrease to a low of 4.9% in October 2016 (compared to a high of 10% in October 2009) employees are increasingly in charge of determining where to work (US Department of Labor 2016). Culture will remain a critical dimension in their choices and in their contentment with their choices.

Let's briefly explain what we mean by culture, how it's measured, and its impact on work fit. By most measures, organizational culture matters to companies and employees for two key reasons:

- It determines the organization's ability to sustain its health over time via performance and results.
- It reflects an employee's daily behaviors, which determine ease of fit and probability of a long-term partnership.

Theories about culture gained popularity in business and management journals in the mid-1900s as organizational development (OD) grew as a field of research and practice dedicated to expanding the effectiveness of people within organizations.

Researchers suggested that organizational culture could significantly affect organizational outcomes, reasoning that culture could be used to affect employee actions, distinguish firms from one another, and create competitive advantage. Organizational cultures start with the values and actions of the company's founders and develop over time as the organization grows and responds to challenges.

Much press has been given in the past 20 years to company perks such as on-site daycare, coffee lounges, dry cleaning services, and nap rooms, which we can think of as artifacts, or visible evidence, of culture. In our experience, these perks are far less important to employees than intangible rewards. Virgin Pulse's (2015) recent study showed that 77% of Millennial workers felt that culture was *more important* than salary and benefits. As Ray Hennessy (2016) said in *Entrepreneur* when he wrote about a company that offered to pay wedding costs as a benefit, "A company with a ping-pong table, ice cream socials, and all-expenses-paid Grub Hub accounts can have lousy culture. Good company culture goes well beyond perks."

Over the last 65 years, as OD theory and practice have evolved, corporate culture has come into focus and is typically defined as the assumptions, values, and behaviors that contribute to the unique environment of a company. Often considered the father of organizational culture theory, Edgar Schein maintained that culture was the most challenging part of a company to change, outlasting products, services, founders, and all physical attributes.

Company values and beliefs are sometimes expressed formally in writing, but whether implicit or explicit, values become evident to employees during work itself.

Cameron recalls when he realized that honesty was of primary importance at his new job. After the team missed a deadline, his boss immediately called the client to inform them of the project schedule change and fully owned the problem. In other jobs, Cameron saw managers fudge to customers about deadlines and deflect accountability. He appreciated his leader staying true to the value of honesty. When your values are aligned with your company's values, it feels like you have a good culture fit.

Just below the values of a company lies the deepest level of organizational culture, the tacit assumptions held between the people who work there, often unseen and not consciously identified in interactions but very much at play (Schein 1990, 112). These are sometimes called *the unwritten rules* of a company, and they explain why there can be paradoxical behaviors within an organization. For example, at a manufacturing company, despite its professed value that "People are the lifeblood of our company," senior leaders' decisions and actions reflected a higher value being placed on expense reduction than on people. When reward and recognition systems were designed and implemented, the company chose lower cost over employee retention, causing high turnover and low engagement.

The gap between professed values and tacit assumptions often makes orientation and assimilation into a company a slow and arduous process for new employees.

Patsy says her situation felt ideal at first. After trying for several years to get hired by a public foundation doing great work, she was thrilled to get a program coordinator job and was relocated to a new city. At first, the culture fit felt great. The foundation's mission was a key driver for all activities, and people were energized and bought into solving big social problems together.

But after the first month, Patsy began to feel some rumblings of trouble. The organization was in a fast-growth mode and often scrambling for funding. This created high adaptability and flexibility, which Patsy appreciated. But she also needed clear and repeated processes. Part of Patsy's work style was to create order, organize, follow rules, and get similar results repeatedly. As she learned the job, she realized the organization was unpredictable and dynamically changing its basic processes. Over time, this created anxiety for Patsy, and after trying to make it work for more than a year, she realized that she needed a job with more structure and clarity to thrive.

There are four attributes of culturally healthy organizations:

- Culture is discussed and examined at the very top.
- The organization has a viewpoint on moral and ethical behavior.
- Internal and external messages are consistent.
- The company embraces transparency.

In unhealthy cultures, these dimensions aren't present, or they're inconsistently applied, which creates stress, anxiety, and frustration for employees.

I've seen four factors that invariably create an unhealthy work culture. Notice if any of these traits are true of your organization because they can point to some things that need to change.

Four Surefire Ways to Mess Up Your Culture

1. **Espouse one set of values while practicing another.** You can have pretty, glossy values statements posted all over your organization's walls, in the employee manual, and tattooed on every leader. However, your organization's day-to-day practices fail to match these values, your employees and your customers will notice. Your company will no longer be trusted. Take the manufacturing company that advertised a safe working environment but hadn't updated their safety procedures to match their new equipment. This company's actions didn't match their stated values.

Instead of feeling safe, employees got the message that what this company valued was the production resulting from the new machinery. Act in accordance with your values, every time.

2. **Tolerate employees who fail to practice the organization's stated values.** Leaders don't always initiate company culture, but they certainly contribute. I can't tell you how often we've discovered pockets of managers within organizations who completely undermined the stated cultural values. Their employees knew it, their customers knew it, and even the managers involved knew it.

    One organization I worked with claimed in posters on the walls that their culture values "inclusion and relentless communication." Yet this same company continuously rewarded a senior VP who almost always failed to involve his team, communicate accurate information, and practice partnership with any of his colleagues. No matter what the organization said about how they did things, this leader didn't model it, and the employees' faith and confidence in the culture was fragile.

    Deal with your managers who haven't bought into the company culture. Hold them accountable and recognize (through compensation, training, or other means) the importance of their roles in creating company culture. Expect them to contribute positively and to embody the organizational culture in their everyday actions. If they can't or won't support the culture, replace them with someone who can and will.

3.   **Have two cultures: One for customers and one for employees.** Employee experiences are customer experiences. I had an experience with an airline attendant that showed what happens in an organization that fails to connect the dots between how they treat their employees and how they treat their customers.

My booked flight had been canceled, so I went to the customer service desk to get another booking. The agent, to quote her more or less, said, "Ma'am, I totally understand what I can do to fix this problem and get you where you want to go, but I'm not authorized to do those things. I suggest you call the 1-800 number to see if the agent you reach has the authority to fix this for you."

This agent knew that treating me well as a customer mattered and that solving problems was her job. She wanted to help me, and knew that her company promise was to help me. But the level of authority she was given limited her ability to help. The dissonance was astounding, and I felt bad for her, bad for me, and bad for the airline, which that day lost my trust as a customer.

Treat your customers and your employees consistently.

4.   **Assume that company culture will take care of itself.** As I mentioned earlier, organizational culture appears as this nebulous, "felt" quality of an organization. As such, it can be easy for leaders to think that if they put the right ingredients into their organizations a healthy culture will emerge. A company I worked with once had

implemented some suggestions they had received about culture, including having beer kegs at work on Fridays and doing personality tests on all its employees. However, they failed to regularly discuss and demonstrate the qualitative elements of the culture they valued (informal professionalism, self-knowledge, work hard/play hard) in their day-to-day work, so employees found the leadership behavior to be inauthentic and rote.

Company culture can be measured, learned, taught, and changed. I've often been called into an organization transitioning from founder to growth stage, but the culture isn't transitioning. Most companies start because someone has an idea or an invention, and they assemble an organization to bring it to the marketplace. The company forms itself around the personality habits and quirks of the founder, who is often more inventor than leader. Over time the culture of how they do things grows to emulate and reinforce how that founder or leader liked to do things. This may work in the early stages, but as people join the company the resultant accidental culture often becomes problematic. For example, a founder who values innovation, may not encourage a culture of consistency. A founder who rules by hierarchy alone may not foster collaboration.

Deliberately deciding how you want to do things in your organization ensures your organization's culture serves your goals and mission. Culture is difficult to build, which is why it needs dedicated focus.

These four surefire ways to mess up your company culture all have something in common. They each show a dissonance between the underlying beliefs of an organization and day-to-day practices. Edgar Schein (1985)[58], a noted organizational culture theorist, has a taxonomy of terms that are quite helpful in diagnosing where these dissonances might occur.

In Schein's framework, the most surface level of culture manifests itself in what he calls the *artifacts* of a company: things that can be seen and felt by an observer, such as facilities, offices, rewards and recognition, titles, policies, attire, slogans, creeds, and published mission/vision statements. Much press has been created in the past 20 years about company perks that all boil down to artifacts: on-site daycare, coffee lounges, dry cleaning services, or nap rooms. While these perks seem meaningful to employees initially, research suggests that, in time, these external perks are less critical than intrinsic rewards, such as success in a role, rich and fun connections with other people, feeling part of something important, and learning. "Nearly nine out of ten, or 86%, Millennials (those between the ages of 22 and 37) would consider taking a pay cut to work at a company whose mission and values align with their own, according to LinkedIn's latest workplace culture report," noted CNBC (Mejia 2018)[59]. While these perks are nice, company culture—that felt presence of an organization—runs much deeper.

Schein called the second level of organizational culture the *professed values*. Unlike a mission statement, these are the values expressed through the *behaviors* of the organization's members. In an organization with a healthy culture, professed values and written company values are often similar. The professed values often lurk unnoticed, but they're apparent in how an organization works. Whether implicit or explicit, those values become evident to employees during their work.

Underneath and informing the professed values are what Schein calls the *tacit assumptions* of the people in an organization. Team members, often unconsciously, tailor their actions to their tacit assumptions. These assumptions are sometimes called the unwritten rules of a company, and they explain why there can be paradoxical behaviors within the organization.

It's often the tension between professed values and tacit assumptions that makes orientation and assimilation to a new company a slow and arduous process for new employees. During this time, they are unwittingly working out the differences between what is professed and what is done, which informs the employees' beliefs about what matters.

As an antidote to the negative examples above, three stories showcase organizational cultures whose three levels are synchronized. In particular, look for these four elements: 1) leaders leading their organization's culture in addition to the mechanics of the business, 2) values at the center, 3) integrity between how things are discussed with employees and how things are done with customers and clients, and 4) transparency, with purpose and no secrets.

- **Story One: Good Customer Service.** On a recent flight, an error was made in my itinerary, and I ended up in somebody else's seat on a full plane. I was told to get off the plane, the last flight of the day, and walk back inside to the desk where they would remedy the situation. When I got to the desk, I was told the plane I'd just been on had left and that I would have to travel home the next day. I was unhappy about this. The representative noticed my agitation and made a call to the plane. She grabbed my paperwork, spoke privately to a colleague, and walked me back down the people carrier. In 10 minutes, I went from feeling annoyed and angry to feeling supported, seen, and cared for by the airline. I could see that the woman helping me was gratified at having been able to give me the assistance I needed. She could do so because she was comfortable seeking assistance from a higher-up for my benefit as a customer.

- **Story Two: Support and Appreciation.** Years ago, I applied for a line of credit for my business. The first bank I approached was a large chain where we had all six of our family accounts. I was told that I needed my husband to co-sign for a business line of credit, even though he was uninvolved in the business. I declined because my husband had no affiliation with my business and walked down the street to a then-new local bank. The manager invited me to a small room and asked how he could help.

I told him my story, and he listened, making notes.

I walked out with my first robust line of credit and a new bank, feeling supported, valued, and appreciated. The manager was motivated to meet my needs, which was his mission. He had a solution, and he knew how to access it.

He was empowered, had apparent authority, understood how to get something done quickly, and empathized with what I needed as a future (and now very loyal) customer.

- **Story Three: Collaboration, Information Sharing, and Empathy.** A client of mine recently suffered a minor car accident on her way to work. She was going to an important meeting and called her boss to say she was delayed because her car needed to be towed. Her boss immediately expressed concern for her welfare. "Was she hurt?" "Did she need help?" And then her boss provided reassurance that her colleagues would cover the meeting.

Because of their team approach, my client wasn't the only person in the know, and the meeting went off flawlessly. Collaboration, information sharing, and empathy were not only company values but actual company practices. When an emergency arose, the company was prepared to handle it.

These successes weren't caused by employees' stand-up desks, free movie passes, nap breaks, unlimited coffee supply, or other surface elements of culture. The people involved acted as they did because they were trained, encouraged, and indoctrinated into a culture that manifested its values, such as customer focus, accountability, team orientation, and problem-solving. These employees understood, consciously or not, the central tenets of the organizations they worked for and knew how to do their work according to these tenets.

At its best, when work is good, culture is unbreakable. It serves the organization day-in and day-out, standing the test of time. When this happens, it is because People Leaders on station cultivate the central elements of culture—they plant the seeds and nurture them regularly.

Healthy, not toxic, culture grows from intention, values, and attention to the realities that culture drives everything.

Endnotes

58 Schein, Edgar H. 1985. *Organizational Culture and Leadership.* San Francisco: Jossey-Bass.

59 Mejia, Zameena. 2018. "Nearly 9 Out of 10 Millennials Would Consider Taking a Pay Cut to Get This." CNBC (June 28).

CHAPTER 14

Plan

Culture is invisible, which is why it can be troubling for organizations.

From the outside, your organization might look incredible— it might even *be* awesome—offering good packages and strong incentives.

But what's it like on the inside?

Decades of research shows that **unhealthy culture is one of the main reasons employees quit.** Yet *healthy* culture is one of the things happy employees most often cite as to *why* they're happy.

The costs of toxic culture are high:

* a high-turnover rate – **you're siphoning revenue to train and re-train.**
* underperforming teams – **work takes too long and is too hard.**
* low employee engagement – **you're paying your employees to scroll Facebook.**

If you've read this far, you might be feeling discouraged.

"Moe, if culture is this invisible, unseen force, what can I do about it?"

This is where I have a piece of good news.

While we can't *see* culture, we know where it comes from and can learn to *Take Charge of Culture*.

It starts with the professed values of the founders.

While the founders (or CEO, top leaders, etc.) set the culture, it develops a life of its own as it trickles down the hierarchy.

What many leaders overlook is the influence *unspoken* values have over culture.

While organizational leaders never say things like "we are trying to create a low trust/toxic company," they may be doing just that by failing to interrupt corrosive behaviors in the company when they occur.

Leaders' **inaction becomes a silent form of consent, quietly affirming the behaviors that erode culture at work.**

Culture is manifested based on what we believe is essential, even if those beliefs contradict your stated values.

If you **claim to value collaboration yet believe in hitting deadlines no matter what, you might be creating a culture that contradicts your values.**

Shaping culture means learning to listen to where your organization's professed values and lived values differ.

This job is the responsibility of leaders at every level, from the bottom to the top.

While culture is tricky to pin down, it's a superpower for leaders who learn to perceive and even shape it in their organization.

Culture is malleable, yet it can live on for generations.

What do you do to keep your team culture healthy and not toxic?

The work of shaping culture begins with *you*, the leader.

It requires sharpening your perceptions and learning to observe how people do things at your organization and what beliefs drive their actions.

Culture is an essential ingredient to making work good. People leaders have a crucial role in shepherding culture as the light that guides the team in the dark. Rather than focusing time and money on surface elements of company culture, leaders of Bravespace workplaces invest resources in developing the people practices that sustain a healthy culture. Usually, this means spending time and money on training, communication, management, and leadership development. Instilling confidence and belief in an organization's core values, and helping people connect the dots between these values and the things they do every day, is what drives strong company culture.

There are no easy fixes, but it helps to have a plan.

Clients frequently ask me, "How long will it take to change our culture"?

It comes from a genuine place.

Leaders are eager to see progress; people are desperate for relief.

And right from the get-go, my clients are relieved to have engaged a consultant for what feels mercurial and intangible.

Full of hope, expectations soar—like at the beginning of January.

In work, as in life, though, there are no easy fixes.

Culture change takes time.

It takes time for people to build trust and understand and believe in the important shifts leaders are making.

As the excitement of the new project wears off, I've found it helpful to stay focused on The Five Pillars of an Unbreakable Culture.

These Five Pillars aren't steps to follow.

They aren't some instantly gratifying panacea.

But, with persistence, they move the needle of your organizational culture slowly closer to thriving.

(One more secret about these pillars: it isn't the pillars themselves that do anything; it's the associated activity, conversation, and behavior change that enlivens and repairs culture.)

The Five Pillars of Unbreakable Culture

1. Follow a People Credo
2. Assess Your Culture
3. Revitalize Your Mission, Vision, and Values
4. Follow a Culture Handbook—not your HR Policy Manual
5. Create a unified Leadership Approach—including DEI

When you get the culture right, here's what people say:

- How [this company] cares about their people really creates the right "vibe" at work, and that makes everyone care about the work/effort they put in.
- [The company] cares very much about the balance of culture and sales focus in employee's lives.
- [This company] finds value in me as a person, an employee, and a leader and I feel empowered to share my thoughts or give feedback.
- I am thriving here!

To summarize, a plan for culture requires these key ingredients:

- **Study your culture.** As the felt quality of an organization, culture often lurks under the surface and takes explicit searching out. Remember that culture is driven by the beliefs, values, and assumptions held by the people who work there. These beliefs, values, and assumptions drive behavior. Look for symbols, rituals, actions, and behaviors, and ask what those tangible practices reveal about a company's culture. This process should reveal both the natural strengths and weaknesses of the company.

  Leadership teams who take the time to either measure their culture with a valid assessment tool, asking employees how they do things, or otherwise openly discuss the beliefs, values, and assumptions that drive behavior in their organization, can realistically assess the often invisible and ignored dimensions of culture that matter.

- **Put culture on the dashboard.** Make sure cultural priorities show up on your strategies, KPIs, performance measures, annual reports and more. What matters gets counted, so put culture on the important to-do lists.

- **Talk about culture.** Whether you measure or try to name your culture, it's important to engage every employee, to find out what they feel and notice about how the company does things. Since culture is a product of the shared beliefs and assumptions of employees, discussion about culture at all levels helps an organization to more specifically connect the dots between what they do today and how they want to be tomorrow. The dissonance between espoused beliefs and values and those in practice becomes a potent lever for change. All employees be engaged in these conversations, rather than just the team at the top, since change will require all employees to begin to think differently to act differently.

- **Take focused action to change.** Interestingly, companies we work with want to start here at this final step. Before change can happen, you need to know the root causes and the culture that exists. Revisit the previous actions.

Pick one to three things at a time to change that will make a difference in your organization's culture. Focus allows all employees to practice new ways of doing things. Trying to consciously rewire tacit assumptions may not always work, but highlighting key practices and behaviors that express those assumptions does.

Here's how one group of leaders does it. During their reflection, this team found that employees often kept silent due to pervasive low trust. The leaders wanted to grow the trust that existed in their workplace and create a less fearful culture. Together, they committed to bringing more heart-based work to how they accomplished things together, and led their teams. In working to build their new leadership team, they have successfully been able to target specific ways to walk their talk and create vulnerability-based trust at all levels. People can engage in ideological debate that's healthy and constructive, which increases performance and job satisfaction.

For example, the leaders now start team meetings with a quick check-in on how people feel. They consciously share the problems or challenges they're facing and the mistakes they've made. They also make it a point to share with the employees the reasons behind the decisions that have been made, practicing the transparency that leads to trust.

This team bravely examined their culture, talked to all their employees about their specific ideas and hopes, and were then poised and ready to act.

Culture is the lifeblood of every organization. It derives from the assumptions we make and the beliefs we hold, and it drives our actions. Bravespace workplace leaders consciously create a culture that mirrors and matches their values.

CHAPTER 15

Purpose

*The greatness of a community is most accurately measured
by the compassionate actions of its members.*

—Coretta Scott King

Why Do You Work?

Every day, most of us choose to get out of bed, get dressed, commute (or don a headset), and pass our day working. We go to work even when we don't want to. According to Barry Schwartz (2015)[60], author of Why We Work, "Ninety percent of adults spend half their waking lives doing things they would rather not be doing at places they would rather not be." Why? We all have our reasons, and the first to roll off our tongues is often "because I have to." In a capitalist society such as ours[61], we need money to take care of ourselves. In the modern age, we trade our time, effort, skills, and experience for cash and other benefits. But, Schwartz notes, it comes down to a higher purpose. Indeed, in my research for Fit Matters, we identified meaning—knowing that what we do matters—as one of six essential elements to a great work fit (Carrick and Dunaway 2017). Which makes sense. As humans, we seek meaning everywhere. So, if we commit our lives to working, we seek meaning from our work.

Workplace research confirms this claim. *Fast Company* (Poswalski 2015)[62] reported that "more than 50 percent of Millennials say they would take a pay cut to find work that matches their values, while 90% want to use their skills for good." We seek ways to matter. But for many of us, meaning at work is missing. According to the Centers for Disease Control and Prevention (Smith 2013)[63], four out of 10 Americans haven't yet discovered a satisfying sense of their purpose. Nearly a quarter of all Americans don't have a sense of what makes their lives meaningful.

In every job held by a human being, a connection to work that's seen by others and makes a difference is important. No matter how entry-level the work, we feel better when we think that the effort we're making makes a difference to someone. It can be as simple as a supervisor who notices extra effort, or a CEO who gives us accountability and room to innovate.

When I talk to clients about this, they sometimes look at me as if my head is upside down. Especially if they make things. "Moe, we sell (insert any object), so our mission is to sell more of it." Got it. But when I say meaning, I don't mean that it is always necessary to save the world. I mean that you should offer to the people who work for you at least one of the following aspects of meaning or purpose:

- **Feeling Seen (I bring something unique, related to me).** Feeling seen means that employees feel that their organization cares about them. Not generically, simply as the person with the training and experience to do a job, but as a unique person with a name and a unique synthesis of qualities and insights that will add unique value. Our human need to belong is tightly connected to feeling seen at work.

In Bravespace workplaces, the people who work there are seen for who they are, in even small ways. People know each other's names. Employees can hang pictures of their beloved people on their walls. Managers give feedback regularly to their employees that helps them learn and lets them know their effort is noticed.

- **Feeling Necessary (What I do matters to someone and has an impact).** I had a client tell me the most devastating story. A new worker at a small manufacturing plant was injured the first week he was on the job, and he was sent home. He had to miss six weeks of work. During that time, only one person called him: HR, who was processing his workers' compensation paperwork. This made him feel like a number in the system. It got worse when he returned to work—no one at the front desk knew where he worked or who his boss was. They asked him to wait in the cafeteria while they sorted it out. No one ever came. He went home, received a paycheck for 12 more weeks, and sought another job. My client, a leader of this organization, only heard this story when the worker called the HR department to tell them to stop paying him because he felt guilty taking money when he wasn't working.

Time and energy are spent in Bravespace workplaces to make sure that every employee, from day one, knows where they fit in the organization's ecosystem. They understand why the work they do matters to the organization overall and what the impact would be if they weren't doing their job.

- **Feeling Occupied (I feel busy and engaged).** Engagement is a popular buzzword for organizations. It measures the extent to which employees feel connected to and stimulated by the company they work for. Have you ever had a job where you watched the clock tick minute after minute? The odds are that if you have, you were barely there. When we feel occupied, time flies by. And when we don't, we find ourselves surfing the web for job openings, fantasizing about better opportunities, and seeking other projects. We find meaning in our jobs when we feel fully occupied by work.

  Bravespace workplaces are designed to make ensure that people have enough to do most of the time. Employees are actively encouraged to think broadly about what they should focus on so that they stay busy and thinking.

- **Feeling Compelled (The organization's products and mission are meaningful to me).** More often, people are looking to hitch their wagon to a company that feeds their value system. They don't want to work just anywhere. A company with a higher-order purpose, that contributes to the world, be it socially, environmentally, or with an innovative product that makes lives better, draws employees who connect to that purpose, and that retains them.

Simon Sinek (2009)[64] speaks about this dynamic in his popular book and TED talk, *Start with Why*.

He says, "If you hire people just because they can do a job, they'll work for your money. But if you hire people who believe what you believe, they'll work for you with blood, sweat, and tears."

Bravespace workplaces have leaders who think about why the organization exists. And those leaders translate the organization's purpose to the role of every person who works for them. Not just once, but often, in a variety of ways.

I consulted with a client who manufactured drywall corners. The CEO asked salespeople to bring videos from the field to HQ to show the office and line staff what it looked like when their products were used in buildings. These short clips of condominiums and art museums all over the country that were beautiful and built safely had the employees who never left their location jumping for joy at their contribution to improving the world.

I will never forget the boss who showed me, when I was 15 years old, what a difference a fresh, hot cup of coffee made to the customers who came to our café on their way to work. And the supervisor for the janitorial job I had when I was 19, who clearly conveyed to me the importance of thoroughly cleaning hospital rooms, so that patients didn't get more ill from their hospital stay. In both those instances, I felt that I was contributing to something, and that my efforts made a difference to someone.

A Reminder About The Sanctity of Work

My late mother, my sister, and I used to share this expression. Sometimes when we're grumpy about having to work on a particularly hard day, we say to each other, "Ah, the sanctity of work. Remember, it's better than the alternative." True on so many levels:

Work gives us a way to contribute. Humans need more than just the air, food, and water we consume. Abraham Maslow refers to those other human needs as self-esteem and self-actualization. Patrick Lencioni calls it our need to do something relevant that makes a difference in the lives of others. A sense of purpose drives us and provides the energy to get us out of bed and to work.

Sometimes, when life gets the best of us, when our personal circumstances are particularly difficult, and work can be a potent distraction that allows us to recover our equilibrium and gain perspective. My sister, whose personal life is packed with high demands from two special-needs sons, finds that her job at a hospital gives her a break of eight or more hours a day from the rigors of her home situation.

- **Work offers relationships.** Even when we struggle with co-workers, having them around forces us to engage. Human beings crave belonging and connection; for many people, work is a primary way to form relationships. Work reduces isolation, and when we see colleagues, hear about their lives, and engage with them in shared tasks and accomplishments, we feel good. Even when they're not our best friends, we look forward to seeing them and being with them.

- **Work stimulates our brains.** Humans like to think. Having to think stimulates us. Jobs that demand creativity, innovation, problem solving, and exploration challenge us. Once we're done with school, work is the logical place we bring and use our powerful brains.

- **Work connects to identity.** Work is a vital dimension of my identity, intertwined with my roles of mother, wife, friend, daughter, athlete, baker, etc. My sense of myself is strongly connected to the work that I do, both paid and unpaid, that makes a difference to someone. At the end of the day, it brings me comfort to know that I have used my assets to do something good or helpful. This is true for most people.

Let's give a thumbs up to the sanctity of work.

Purpose Matters

We got to work to make money because we live in a capitalist society, and money is how we support ourselves. But what makes work good is feeling a higher purpose there.

As Viktor Frankl said, "Ever more people today have the means to live, but no meaning to live for." When work is good, we find a reason to be there that matters to us, gives us meaning, and adds purpose to why we exist.

Endnotes

60   Schwartz, Barry. 2015. *Why We Work*. New York: Simon and Schuster, TED Books.

61   Note that the phrase *to spend one's time* directly implies that time operates like money. It also implies that time is finite, that we only have so much of it.

62   Poswolsky, Adam Smiley. 2015. "What Millennial Employees Really Want." *Fast Company* (June 4). https://www. fastcompany. com/3046989/what-millennial-employees-really-want.

63   Smith, Emily Esfahani. 2013. "There's More to Life Than Being Happy." *The Atlantic* (January 9).

64   Sinek, Simon. 2009. *Start with Why*. New York: Simon and Schuster, TED Books.

CHAPTER 16

Actions for Sustaining
an Unbreakable Culture

For Leaders or Business Owners

Plant

- Consider yourself a cultural petri dish: whatever grows inside of you will grow in your company. Do what you say you want done. Show up. Be real.
- Expect your leaders to walk the talk and hold them accountable when they do things inconsistent with the culture.
- Share how you deal with your vendors and partners. Watch how they do things, and ensure their culture and yours align.
- Weave DEIB into every practice, partnership, and policy in your company or organization.

Plan

- Study your culture and put it into words.
- Measure your culture; there are many effective tools for surveying culture in the marketplace.
- Share the results with employees and talk about what it means to them.
- Examine how people experience your culture from different identity groups (based on race, gender, sexual orienta-

tion, ability, and more) to examine equity, inclusion, and belonging honestly.

Purpose
- Spend time thinking about and writing down why your business exists beyond the marketing tagline. Why does the world need you? What difference does your organization make?
- Challenge every leader on your team to connect the purpose of your organization to every person who works for them.
- Connect your customers' experiences to your employees' experiences. They feed off each other and are two sides of the same coin.
- Learn how to share context in both directions—with your board, shareholders, and investors on the one hand and your employees at all levels on the other. Learn how to share it simply and clearly.
- Think about your why: Why are you in your role? Why did you start this company? Tell the story repeatedly.

For Employees

Plant
- Participate in culture assessments and be honest.
- Consider yourself a cultural ambassador; spread the word.
- Speak up when you see people acting in ways that undermine the culture.
- Explore what it means to partner for inclusion and ally across different identities.

Plan
- Think about what you do to contribute to your company's cultural health.
- Spend time exploring your identity and why it matters to the culture you are part of.

Purpose
- Know your why—beyond pay
- Take time to understand why you choose to work at this place. What difference does it make?
- Consider the reason that your organization exists. Ask yourself if you can support this reason and how.
- Talk about the good stuff that work brings you.

For Human Resources or People Development (if they exist in your company)

Plant
- Make it your job to keep culture in front of the leadership.
- Don't think that you own the culture—it's not yours alone.
- Invest in data gathering about how culture is perceived across different demographics in the organization to learn about people's actual felt experience.

Plan
- Examine how what you do represents your company's culture.
- Make yourself more of a cultural steward than a compliance officer.

- Find the right tool(s) so your organization can measure regularly.
- Build straightforward ways to design policies and practices that are equitable and inclusive.

Purpose
- Make sure that new hires are vibrantly on board so that they understand from the beginning why the company exists and what their part in it is.
- Emphasize *Why?* in recruiting practices and documents.
- Challenge yourself to meet the needs of your employees beyond your role in compliance and administration.
- Train managers at all levels to connect meaning to their leadership practices.

PART V

Activate Teams
Who Care

CHAPTER 17

Courage, Care, and Conflict

The worst team I was ever on didn't get me. The company hired me, and I was thrilled. It was a cutting-edge technology company, and I was eager to show them my stuff. What I experienced when I got there was demoralizing. There was no room for my strengths and weaknesses; I felt that all I had were weaknesses. What made it even worse was that my peers seemed to be experiencing success after success. Our meetings were a game of one-upmanship. My colleagues' projects were all completed on time and budget, while mine, which weren't going as well, became the focus of every meeting. "How can you do better, Moe?" It wasn't long before my optimism and energy had eroded to frustration and anxiety. I changed from eager and curious to fearful and secluded, merely following a to-do list, my creative spark gone. It didn't take long for me to search and happily commit to another firm. Back then, I didn't know what made teams click, so I assumed I was the problem.

In my work, I see countless individuals thinking the same thing: "My job sucks, and it seems like it's all my fault." I'm here to say that it's *not* always your fault. Some teams work and some teams that don't. In this chapter, I'll combine research, a whole lot of experience, and strategies for heart-based leading, and closely examine what makes a team brave and how you can help your team thrive.

What Makes a Good Team?

The elements of an effective team have been studied extensively over the last 75 years. Early researchers believed that teams just got better over time as referenced in Bruce Tuckman's model (1965)[65], where teams naturally progress through predictable stages (forming, storming, norming, performing). More recent models, such as Patrick Lencioni's (2002), understand that team health takes more work than mere patience. Lencioni asserts that vulnerability-based trust is a keystone of healthy team development. Google's Aristotle Project (Rozovsky 2015)[66] and Thomas Malone's MIT research (Wolley and Malone 2011) can be consolidated into three common characteristics of high-performing and healthy teams[67]. The first characteristic is equal airtime: groups that solved problems well together paid attention when someone spoke and shared the time roughly equally, with no one dominating. Relatedly, the Aristotle Project revealed the importance of psychological safety: people weren't fearful of harm or recrimination when they shared, they took more risks with the support of the group. The second is social sensitivity: the members of groups that performed well were in tune with each other, noticed subtle shifts in mood and demeanor, and were alert to and responsive to one another's needs. Third, Malone's research showed that the teams that performed best with complex problems contained more women. This may be because women are socialized more toward feminine values—connectedness, empathy, trustworthiness, balance, etc.—discussed in Gerzema and D'Antonio's The Athena Doctrine cited earlier.

My work affirms these findings. Healthy teams are the ones whose members share a mission and listen to and appreciate one another. I work with teams desperate to reach this level of success. I often see teams trying creative things such as bringing cupcakes on birthdays, kegs of beer on Fridays, or hosting events such as fire walking or team paintball. While these activities can be fun[68], they usually don't deepen the relationships of the team members in the heart-based way that healthy teams need. One problem with these sorts of events is that they often alienate the introverts in the group, who might find socializing exhausting. Another is that they tend to lead to superficial connections at best. As business leader and best-selling author Margaret Heffernan (2015)[69] says: Social capital [the ability of a team to grow the trust, knowledge, and shared norms that make healthy groups] isn't about chumminess. It doesn't mean work colleagues have to become best pals or that good cheer is a permanent requirement. Many of the greatest teams are scratchy, sharing impatience with anything less than the best.

Grumpy orchestras tend to play better than cheerful ones; they're focused on performing better, and happiness is the output, not the input, of their work together. In organizations with high degrees of social capital, disagreement doesn't feel dangerous; it is taken as a sign that you care; the best-thinking partners don't confirm your opinions but build on them. They know every idea starts flawed, incomplete, or downright bad. In organizations with high degrees of social capital, conflict, debate, and discussion are how it gets better.

When team-building activities aren't designed to build team health and develop social capital, they flop, leaving people

happy for the cupcake, but no closer to increasing the health of their team. Leaders who make work good instead foster team health by intentionally building brave teams. That is, teams need to study what makes a good team generally, but more importantly, they need to reflect on what makes the members of their teams thrive. Reflecting on the following four questions about trust, conflict, team dynamics, and courage will help your team develop their social capital and become that grumpy but effective orchestra that Heffernan envisioned.

An Equation to Remember

When it comes to team health, both individual well-being and team well-being matter. We consider this an equation: Self-Care + Team Care = A Healthy Cohesive Community.

Self-Care is the critical work we must do to take care of our total well-being; when we don't, we have less capacity, energy, and excellence to bring to work.

The SHELTER Model of Self-Care helps employees remember what is included in good self-care practice.

Sleep: "Routinely sleeping less than six or seven hours a night demolishes your immune system… disrupts blood sugar levels… increases the likelihood of your coronary arteries becoming blocked… [and] contributes to all major psychiatric conditions, including depression, anxiety, and suicidality." If this quote from Matthew Walker's *Why We Sleep* doesn't scare you into sleeping more, maybe try getting good sleep for a week or two and see how good it feels. Treat it as a holy ritual.

Hydrate: Most of our bodies are water. A good target is one fluid ounce per pound of body weight.

Eat: Our bodies need macro and micronutrients to fuel good thinking and high energy. Ideally, from natural sources as much as possible.

Love: Humans are hard-wired for connection. Tend to your friends and beloved ones and turn to them for support and care. It matters.

Take In Air: The data on this is so clear. Breathing in and out deeply a few times a day rekindles self-compassion, reduces stress hormones, and helps us cope. Certain smartwatches can be set up to prompt you into calm breathing throughout the day. For more information, check out *Breath* by James Nestor.

Exercise: Move your body. Ideally, you move throughout the day, getting at least 150 minutes of "endurance-like" activity weekly.

Rest: Why have sleep and rest on the list twice? Because they're different things. Non-Sleep Deep Rest can be performed periodically throughout the day and helps increase learning, calmness, creativity, and more.

So, if you're having an off day, remember to check in on the status of your SHELTER. When you take care of yourself, you elevate your capacity to care for anyone or anything else.

But, Self-Care alone is not enough. The interconnection of everyone in the workplace makes work good by ensuring that others are tending to the well-being of the team as well. When we extend ourselves to assist, support, and nurture others with whom we work, the team is strengthened (and, by the way, we feel better.) We envision this as a Wheel of Team Care where the people leader is the hub, the team members are the spokes, and the rim is the connective tissue between team members that keeps the wheel rolling.

The Wheel of Team Care

People leaders who tend to the health of the rim (the relationships between team members) reduce the dependence the team has on them as the leader to solve problems, reduce the toxic costs of gossip and triangulation, encourage candor and co-commitment, and create an environment where everyone feels included.

Is There Trust in Your Work Situation?

The dynamics of a workplace can often interrupt the formation of vulnerability-based trust. Competition that pits employees against each other ensures that they'll look at each other suspiciously. These environments, where trust and respect don't exist between colleagues, almost always work out poorly. Politics, power-mongering, competition, and subtle discounting behaviors degrade the faith and confidence of colleagues and create hidden and/or public tensions.

The evolution of healthy work relationships is proportional to the trust and mutual respect that are nurtured between people. When we feel connected, we feel safe, so we're willing to be vulnerable, and courageously speak our truth, which elevates others' ability to trust us—and the cycle perpetuates itself. In trusting relationships, we can make mistakes, learn, and grow—without fear of judgment or recrimination. In the workplace, trust between colleagues is a critical element of team cohesion.

Look at this list of traits common to highly trusting teams— teams composed of people who have invested in creating positive, healthy, trust-based relationships at work—and ask yourself which you see at your job and which you don't.

- Individuals talk openly about their strengths and their weaknesses.
- People offer support and challenges in meetings, clarifying their intentions and asking questions without appearing judgmental.
- People know more about each other than just their names.
- People are seen to be valuable beyond their output. Maybe there are references around the office to people's lives outside the workplace (images, artwork, etc.).
- People assume positive and generous intentions in their interactions with one another.
- Competition is focused on winning in the market or against the competition rather than internally. When we win, we win together.
- Team leaders and people managers walk the talk—they do what they say should be done.
- In meetings, sharing and listening are distributed evenly.
- People admit to their mistakes and discuss their learning opportunities.

The presence of vulnerability-based trust is the baseline for all the work that brave teams can accomplish together. Bravespace workplace leaders spend the time and effort to teach, model, and practice with their people how to bake trust into all interactions that teams have with one another every day.

Does Your Team Engage in Healthy Conflict?

Unhealthy conflict saps a workplace. Moreover, the shrapnel of unresolved conflict can stymie, stunt, and stop the work at hand. The ability of people at work to move from conflict to resolution is a key determinant of team health. Conflict, when we work through it, is a positive thing. It opens the possibility of extreme growth. Healthy conflict invites innovation, inspires creative problem-solving, sows hope, and deepens trust. In dynamic, healthy workplaces, people disagree, have ideological differences, and confront divergent points of view, and they do so with their heart skills. Some essential elements that are present in conflict-healthy workplaces include:

- People challenge each other's ideas in meetings without hesitation because they know that this challenge will be regarded as the challenge of an idea and not a person's judgment. Issues are left on the table until they're resolved, and all participating parties are satisfied.
- When people disagree, it's done with respect.
- People tell the truth, even when it's hard. They are vulnerable.
- Leaders model healthy conflict with their colleagues and with their teams.
- There are no gossipy "meetings after meetings" because people are forthright with their feelings.

In my work with clients, four themes have come up repeatedly when it comes to healthy teams. They all have to do with having hard conversations at work. Things like giving people feedback and speaking our truth. And I feel you. Talking about tough things at work—or home—is hard. But guess what? The alternative is to keep your misery, judgement, fear, resentment, and insecurity tucked down deep, where it will rot and fester until one day it leaks out and boom:

…you have a stress-related illness.

…you're yelling at your colleague.

…you can't take it any longer and quit.

But how, Moe? How can I talk about the stuff I don't know how to share?

Let's break down the four most common lies we tell ourselves about having hard conversations at work.

Each lie stems from a story we tell ourselves. It's a false story, though, because something more happening beneath our awareness.

For each story, I'll show you how it's a lie, give you suggestions for getting honest with yourself, and then tell you what to do about it.

As I go through each story, ask yourself, when was the last time I told myself this story? How can understanding the lie help me build stronger relationships?

The first story: "I am afraid to give [person] feedback because I don't want to hurt/offend them."

The Lie:

Most of us make up a story that our colleagues can't handle our truth and will crumble underneath the message we want to convey. Get real, Johnny. Human beings are incredibly resilient, especially when we feel someone is giving us important feedback about impact. What's going on here is that you don't want to be rejected, hurt, or left behind. We fear disconnection more than we fear just about anything. It drives us to keep our feedback silent even when it would help.

Your reality check:
Remind yourself that the story you're making up—that they will resent, hate, or leave you because of your feedback—is likely not true. Admit to yourself that it feels scary to tell them the truth because you care. Be honest with yourself that you have something at stake: you want to be in this relationship with them at work or home. There is no guarantee that sharing your feedback will help, but I can promise you that staying silent will hurt both of you. Get grounded in why you want to share the feedback.

What you can do:
- Set the stage for your feedback: "Because I care about you, I have some feedback. Would you like it?
- Be clear: "When you [their action], I felt [emotion]. I wanted you to know because I am sure you did not mean to have that impact."
- Remind them that you appreciate them listening and support their continued growth.

Examples:
- "When you were late for our meeting, I felt disrespected."
- "When you shared the team's contributions but forgot to include me on the slide, I felt unseen."
- "When you missed our one-on-one meeting three times in a row, I felt nervous and made up the story that you don't want to meet with me because I am about to be fired."

- "When you interrupted me in the group meeting, I felt my opinion didn't matter."

The second story: "I'm afraid of the repercussions if I tell my boss what I really think, so I don't bother."

The Lie:

Imagine your worst fear. What evidence do you have that it is likely to happen? What are you believing here? Will you get fired for telling your boss the truth? It's one thing if there's a track record of people in power mistreating those beneath them who speak truth. These cases are rare, though. More often than not, it's the same base fear as the first story: you value the relationship and don't want to break it. Of course, if you plan to sling judgmental accusations like a scene from *The Office*, that could be hard for your boss to hear. But telling them the truth when they need it to be effective? That is priceless.

Your reality check:

Stop making sh*t up. Ask yourself, is this likely? Which is more risky, speaking your truth or continuing to stifle yourself and complain about your boss to other people? Is this side-talk helping? Okay, time to get brave.

What you can do:

- Get grounded in the truth and your courage.
- Follow the steps from the first story to have an authentic and vulnerable conversation with your boss.

The third story: "How can I have hard conversations when there is no base of trust with someone?"

The Lie:
It is false to believe that trust is a zero-sum game. Our cup is not full or empty when it comes to trust, but constantly evolving in layers. If you lack trust, a vulnerable and hard conversation will add a layer. It'll build trust, so start now.

Your reality check:
Remember that vulnerability is the fastest way to build trust. That's right, the fastest. Give a little, get a lot. Lead the way. Be vulnerable first, don't wait around for them. How do you do that? By leaning into the uncertainty, risk, and emotional exposure you feel.

What you can do:
- Be honest with your internal experience: say, "The story I am making up is [the story you've made up]. Is that accurate?"
- Listen to their response. It will either be, "Oh my gosh, no, that is not true, here is what is…" OR, "You know what, that is true. Let's talk about it." Either way, you are better off knowing what is real.

Examples:
- "The story I am making up is that when you didn't assign me to tackle that project, it is because you think I am incompetent?"
- "The story I am making up is that you think I am overwhelmed because you keep asking if I need help."

- "The story I am making up is that because you gave Mary that promotion, I am going nowhere here in our company."

The fourth story: "They should know better."

The Lie:
Just think about this one. Consider it for a moment. If they knew better or understood the implications, don't you think they would be doing something differently?

Your reality check:
Don't be arrogant. Imagine they have not been given the truth before or have not understood and don't know better? Imagine that they are doing the best they can. Would that change how you feel? Be more generous. You can do that.

What you can do:
- When you feel yourself reacting in indignation or anger, take a few breaths.
- Imagine it from their perspective.

Are you starting to see the theme?

There is a larger narrative beneath each of the common complaints we make about our relationships at work there is a larger narrative. A more generous, honest way of communicating.

A world where these techniques and reframes are pervasive would be an easier world for all of us.

How Big is Your Team?

Copious research confirms that productivity is highest in teams with four to twelve members (Brodzinksi 2014)[70]. Teams with fewer than four members end up functioning more like partners without the desired synergistic lift of team cohesion and elements such as innovation, feedback, creativity, and productivity. On the other hand, teams with more than twelve members become unwieldy. Big teams see communication breakdown, disengagement, and division into dysfunctional sub-teams. Based on my experience working with hundreds of teams over the last 30 years, I'd say the sweet spot is between eight to twelve members, with fluctuations allowable.

Although size matters when creating impactful teams, it's secondary to establishing a team purpose; clear guidelines and expectations for individual contributions; ongoing, team-focused investment and feedback; and a defined leadership structure.

How Courageous Are You and Your Teammates?

Working in a small, trusting, conflict-healthy team is scary. People often cite fear as the central struggle when having difficult conversations at work. Their thoughts include, "I don't want to hurt them," "I fear offending them," or "I don't want to alienate them and lose the relationship." Even when we know the benefits of honest feedback—healthy conflict, innovation, creativity, and deepened trust—the fear of either being hurt ourselves or hurting the receiver causes us to avoid or dilute the vital message we have.

Old definitions of courage focused on mental or moral strength to venture, persevere, and withstand danger, fear, or difficulty.

A new kind of courage (from Dr. Brené Brown) is showing up and letting yourself be seen, despite the risk.

Showing up and letting ourselves be seen is central to the creation of healthy teams through vulnerability-based trust, which is the essential ingredient upon which we can successfully talk about hard things with colleagues at work.

Adapted from the work of Gordon Barnhart (2018)[71], these four types of courage can help us remain centered and focused during difficult conversations:

- **Courage to See and Speak the Truth.** There must be something to discuss before we can have a difficult discussion. We must foster the courage to see the (often difficult) truth. Once we see it, we can name what's happening between us. By learning to see and speak the truth, we can mend problems or create new solutions. Being a truth teller means authentically verbalizing what we see to others, despite our worry that it might offend. It helps to remember that the truth we speak is true for us—the other person may not see it that way.

- **Courage to Create and Hold Forth a Vision of the Desired State.** This form of courage invites us to imagine ourselves and the other person successfully on the other side of the difficult conversation. Holding an image of getting through the conversation intact and in strong partnership can guide the conversation. With a vision of a positive outcome, our fears are less likely to usurp and break down the conversation. It can also be an excellent way to articulate intention. Don't look at where you are, but where you want to go. Positive outcomes are more likely if you have a successful resolution and an even stronger partnership clearly in mind, and you don't let fear guide and derail the conversation.

- **Courage to Persevere and Hold the Course.** The intense feelings during a difficult conversation can threaten the entire interaction. We must hang on even when the exchange gets stormy, trusting that on the other side of our differences is a successful resolution wherein we understand each other and feel that we have honestly expressed ourselves, listened, and been heard. A mindfulness practice that teaches the discipline of the mind and patience in uncomfortable situations can aid in one's ability to persevere.

- **Courage to Collaborate with and Rely On Others.** Ultimately, difficult conversations aren't conversations; they're interactions. Suppose we're in a feedback exchange or difficult conversation with another person. In that case, it's because both of us matter to the outcome—the partnership itself is consequential to the eventual outcome. We have each contributed to the problem and the solution. Telling ourselves that we can do it alone usually fails to garner and offer the support we need to do an excellent job. Our ability to foster interdependence creates an environment in where we can accomplish phenomenal things.

Developing these courageous habits in your team can encourage the development of healthy feedback and ways to communicate.

Listening to the Music

Live music performed well is the ultimate example of team performance in action. Annually, my husband and I head up the road to the Sisters Folk Festival, an event in our home community that showcases musicians from around the world. Inspired by these artists, I have made a list of the top five things you can do to create a Bravespace workplace that will move your group from *barely getting by* to *achieving amazing results together*:

1. **Listen first.** Great musicians watch and listen to one another acutely. As they play, someone goes first, and the others fill in behind based on what they hear and what's needed. When someone decides to do a riff or change a scale, the others are tuned in to catch it and respond instantaneously. Although some take the spotlight, they are enabled to do so by their bandmates. *In the teams you work with, are you listening to the others? Do you listen first to try to understand? Or are you so busy with your work that you fail to notice the others?*

2. **Know your part.** Some musicians pluck, some bang, some blow—each voice, each instrument, and each player has a specific contribution to the whole that is, in fact, the point. *In your team, are you crystal clear on what your part is? Do you know what it takes to give your best performance to the team? Do you have the self-awareness to understand*

what your greatness looks like and how you can deliver it repeatedly to your team?

3. **Be vulnerable and imperfect.** I once saw a singer performing a new song. She was eager to share and proud of it, but because it was new, she needed to use her iPhone to recall the lyrics. She took a risk in trying something new publicly, and she was honest with herself that it would be best if she sacrificed the appearance of professionalism for a genuine performance of her new song. It was a beautiful song.

   Putting yourself out there with your sound, voice, and ideas requires an awareness that it may not be perfect, but it will still be right. If this musician hadn't performed out of fear that she might forget the lyrics, we wouldn't have heard it. If team members never risk, teams stay predictable, static, and slow. *What is scary for you to say to your team members? What ideas do you have that you hold back from sharing? What might happen if you jump in and take a risk before you have it all perfectly worked out? What tools can you use to help manage your fear so that you can take risks bravely?*

4. **Have a plan.** Musicians on stage invariably have a song list they follow, that little slip of paper they tuck under a drum or in their pocket that reminds them of what the plan is for the set. The band knows the plan and has rehearsed the flow in order to be ready to perform each song in order. *Does your team have clarity on why it exists? Do you each know what the outcomes are and what the timing is? Can every member tell you how the team is progressing?*

5. **Be willing to go off plan.** Planning doesn't always cut it. Take the young songwriters I saw who unexpectedly joined a seasoned expert, the musician who plucked a violin when his mandolin broke, or the time the audience was suddenly asked to sing the refrain and created a magnificent harmony with the lead singer. *Are you willing to vary from the plan with your team when something comes up? Can you discard your solid strategy when it doesn't work and be nimble and responsive?*

At some point in our lives, most of us are fortunate enough to experience what true team cohesion feels like, yet thinking deeply about the part we play in making this happen is often relegated to off-time and accidental reflection. Take time to listen to the music. Notice how talented artists can create the ultimate synergistic lift and cohesion. Identify your part and the other parts that align to create powerful teams that can achieve phenomenal results.

Bravespace workplace teams spend time and energy fortifying their individual and collective partnership skills.

They know that what they each know is less important than what they learn together, and their priority and focus remain on the success of all.

Endnotes

65 Tuckman, B. W. 1965. "Developmental Sequence in Small Groups." *Psychological Bulletin, 63* (6), 384–99.

66 Rozovsky, Julia. 2015. "The Five Keys to a Successful Google Team." Re:*Work* (November 17). Google. https://rework. withgoogle. com/blog/five-keys-to-a-successful-google-team/.

67 In Malone's research, individual IQ and aggregate IQ had no effect on a group's ability to solve complex problems, again suggesting that teams need heart skills and not head skills.

68 Gallup's research (2017b) suggests that having friends at work is one of the top 12 contributors to job satisfaction, but a healthy team environment is less about being friends (socially) than about being able to relate to others in a way that makes us feel seen and connected.

69 Heffernan, Margaret. 2015. *Beyond Measure: The Big Impact of Small Changes.* New York: Simon and Schuster, TED Books.

70 Brodzinksi, Pawel. 2014. "The Fallacy of the Ideal Team Size." *Software Project Management* (January 28). http://brodzinski. com/2014/01/ideal-team-size-fallacy.html.

71 Barnhart, Gordon. 2018. *Center for Heroic Leadership.* http:// www. heroicleaders.com

CHAPTER 18

Actions to Activate
Teams Who Care

For Leaders or Business Owners

- Note that not all work groups are teams. Does your team share a common purpose? What is it? It's usually better to invest in teams with a compelling and specific reason to partner.
- Create an environment of safety by having shared norms for how the team members behave together, including how they share airtime. How will you tell each other when one of you has talked too much?
- Design ways to invite vulnerability. Ask people to share mistakes that they've made. Invite personal stories that help team members to see one another in richer ways.
- Go first with vulnerability. As the leader, what you do goes a thousand times further than what you say they should do.
- Commit to occasional rest and play. It creates resilience.
- Invite and practice healthy conflict.
- Ask personal questions that probe at the emotional underpinnings of decision-making. Instead of asking, "What problems do you see with this plan?" ask, "What about this plan makes you uncomfortable?" "Why?"
- Turn up the dial on feelings: name, share, and validate them with empathy. Sharing and making room for the

emotions at play between people helps them to feel safe and tune in to one another.

- Host occasional team advances[72], in which you and your team celebrate, play, plan, and connect. These are best when they're away from the office and when they inspire or delight in any small way.
- Invest time and space for teams to build their relationships with each other—the rim of the team care wheel.
- Name and navigate team differences in race, gender, ability, and more. Lean into not away from the hard conversations.

For Employees

- Know yourself, your role, what makes your heart sing, and what your best qualities are for any team you serve.
- Learn about difficult conversations and have them. Notice the things that you're feeling but not saying. Say those things.
- Invest time developing relationships with your colleagues through genuine connection.
- Think of feelings as a data source and share them with an open heart.
- Practice empathy.
- Educate yourself about your identity, why it matters, and partnering with people who are different.

For HR or People Development (if they exist in your company)

- Offer tools that help teams to start well, such as designed experiences, kick-offs, assessments, or team advances.
- Point employees back to their peers when they come to you with complaints or issues. "Have you and Sue tried to sort this out? If so, have you tried . . .?" Help them to work it out themselves.
- Offer programs that build skills to have difficult conversations. Train your people in heart-based leadership.
- Support leaders in maintaining team health.
- Require the senior team to be brave.
- Survey more often, using pulse survey tools such as Waggl, Survey Monkey, or any tool that allows you to frequently get the inputs of your employees about how leaders and teams are doing.
- Give teams tools and support for building equitable and inclusive practices.

Endnote

72   We prefer the term team advance rather than the traditional *retreat,* which wrongly suggests going backward.

PART VI

Complexities

CHAPTER 19

AI, Machines, and Robots, Oh My!

In a properly automated and educated world, then, machines may prove to be the true humanizing influence. It may be that machines will do the work that makes life possible and that human beings will do all the other things that make life pleasant and worthwhile.

—Isaac Asimov, *Robot Visions*

In my first job after grad school, the CEO of my company, Craig McCaw, a leader in the burgeoning cellular (before digital!) revolution, held an all-employee meeting and said that he believed that one day we would do everything from our phones: banking, email, movies, route-finding. Everything. He said that someday we might not even need the phones because we would have implants in our heads that did it all. Frankly, we, the lowly workers, thought he was out of his mind. We had just gotten used to the idea that our phones didn't need to be plugged into the wall, and anyone wanting a "cell" phone was stuck carrying around a chunk of plastic the size of a bunch of celery.

But look at us now. Over three-quarters of the US population own smartphones (Pew Research Center 2018)[73]. I use What's App to talk to my daughter in Buenos Aries. I order take-out, schedule the dog groomer, order meal tickets, plan my vacation, and look for an exercise class on this little device. Despite the challenges of the profit-based capitalist consumerist culture we live in that I mentioned in Chapter 1, we have this culture to thank for the development and mass production of our cherished devices. The world of work is full of paradoxes.

As most of us know, technological advances are speeding up. Many experts say that the issue is not whether technology will *speed* up, but whether we human beings will *keep* up. Since the 1960s, American technologists have been speculating about the possibility of an intelligence explosion brought on by the invention and distribution of super-intelligent computers. The thinking goes that after this hypothetical moment, often called the technological singularity, humans will be outpaced, outnumbered, or even ruled by machines. Films such as *I, Robot*, *The Matrix*, or the *Terminator* series are science-fiction predictions of this moment. For many theorists, a pivotal moment will be the development of computers that can pass the Turing test.

The Turing test, popularized in the award-winning 2014 film *The Imitation Game*, is a test named after its creator, the brilliant Alan Turing (1950)[74], and a thought experiment he invented in his seminal paper, "Computing Machinery and Intelligence." The Turing test is a relatively simple exercise designed to determine whether or not a theoretical machine has intelligence indistinguishable from a human's.

What many people overlook, however, is an earlier paper by Turing (1937)[75] called "On Computable Numbers, with an Application to the Entscheidungsproblem." Although the paper is esoteric—it's written for professional logicians—the implications of this paper are arguably more significant than his discussion of the popularized Turing halting problem.

I'll skip over the math—a subject worthy of its own book—to summarize the significance of Turing's work to the creation of Bravespace workplaces. Turing's paper proves that no possible algorithm could determine the solvability of a given problem – there is no algorithm that can say whether a given problem has or doesn't have a solution. Proving this, Turing invented a "machine" whose functioning forms the theoretical basis for today's computer processors, and proving this machine cannot answer specific questions.[76] Interestingly, a consequence of Turing's paper is that humans can determine whether or not a given equation has a solution, even if it's difficult to find. In other words, Turing simultaneously invented and proved the limits of computational thinking. Today's computers, super-computers, and quantum computers must follow the rules of logic that underlie Turing's proof: there are and always will be some things that humans can do that machines cannot. Yet despite this proof, and perhaps because of its inaccessibility, much popular media focuses on the threat posed by the abundance of machines in today's workplaces.

Fear of this threat is justified since workers have been and continue to be replaced by machines that can perform their labor more efficiently and for longer periods, without fatigue, and can compute vast amounts of data much more quickly. The

McKinsey Global Institute (2018)[77] predicts that as early as 2030, robots and AI will force up to one-third of the American workforce to switch to new occupations.

As Turing proved, there are some jobs that humans will always do. This leaves us not so much with the question of the fate of humanity as machines take over but rather the problem of how to organize and work with machines to find the right and best role for everyone—human or machine. As Kevin Drum (2017)[78] said in Mother Jones, "Until we figure out how to fairly distribute the fruits of robot labor, [we are facing] an era of mass joblessness and mass poverty."

What is it that humans can do that robots can't? And how do we ensure that our job economy uses each of these resources to the fullest? Leaders should be asking three key questions today that will shape tomorrow's workplace regarding technology trends. What work is unique to humans? What role does work play in the health of society? How can machines reinforce what humans do best?

Here are some of the important things that AI cannot do at work:

- Express emotions
- Show empathy
- Be creative
- Have a conscience
- Make moral or ethical decisions
- Have a sense of humor

Work That's Unique to Humans

Turing proved that no machine could decide the solvability of a given math problem, but a person can. But that doesn't mean we should all become mathematicians seeking to determine solvability. Most experts agree that there is one area of human cognition that machines may never emulate – human connection. Getting the mix of pheromones, hormones, body language, intuition, emotions, and so on just right in a machine will be extremely difficult and has proved impossible. Imagine, for a moment, a machine comforting you in the doctor's office after a devastating diagnosis, when you most need someone to empathize with the shock and pain you feel. Or a robot motivating and inspiring a group of programmers to stay up all night to reach a deadline, when every fiber of their being thinks it's crazy. These and countless other scenarios require nuanced, unique human contemplation, reflection, communication, and impact that is likely impossible for a machine of any type to replicate.

What's more, our need for loving, emotional, wholehearted contact with other human beings is as important to us as food, water, air, and shelter; in fact, we connect very well. We bring our need and talent for connection with other human beings into every aspect of our lives, including work. This need drives much about how we live together in communities, at work and at home.

As AI and robots proliferate, a key echelon of work will endure. All the jobs requiring empathy, care, compassion, and connection, such as teaching, childcare, social work, nursing, counseling, primary care, leadership, and even customer service will be relevant in a robotic future. At present, many of these jobs are found at the bottom of the wage and desirability pile. Still, in a machine-fueled future, we might see increased demand and compensation for positions requiring intimate human connection.

All organizations should know which of their roles fall in the "uniquely human" realm and consider how they will recruit, develop, and reward people to grow their skill and fluency in these jobs. People are not machines, which is good for any job requiring human connection, inspiration, collaboration, leadership, trust, creativity, and intuition.

The Role Work Plays in the Overall Health of Society

What businesses do and how they do it impacts spheres of our lives beyond the walls of a conference room. It is critical that we not limit our thinking about the role of working machines to merely replacing jobs. As jobs change, we see reverberant changes in the social construct of "work"—a construct relevant to the total health of our families, neighborhoods, cities, nation, and our world. Figuring out how our two general types of workers—machines and humans—are structured in our economies will determine whether each category is beneficial or detrimental to our society. First, workers make money. Money buys food, shelter, and other commodities. The activity of buying things fuels economic growth—Economics 101. But if a robot takes my job, the whole system crumbles. I have no money to spend. As a result, the people around me stop getting paid, and so on. A simple change—the massive redistribution of the demand for employment – changes the global structure of economics.

Business owners, shareholders, and leaders must think deeply about which currencies they exchange with workers. What do you offer as an employer that matters to your workers? The complex bundle of cash, benefits, paid time off, meaning, a place to go, relationships, the ability to grow, etc. must be considered to elevate and reward people at work tomorrow.

We work for money to buy food, shelter, and sometimes candy. But, and this is my second point, we also work because it makes us matter. From ancient Greek philosopher Aristotle's *Nicomachean Ethics*, which states that work makes life meaningful, to Barry Schwartz's book, *Why We Work*, we're told that when we contribute to something or someone outside of ourselves, our purpose motivates us to keep going.

What happens to our drive for community if people can't work? Or our eagerness to continue? As portrayed in Pixar's computer-animated science fiction hit *WALL-E*, our life force likely atrophies and dies, leaving in its wake social problems, including addiction, crime, family failures, depression, and the failure of social networks. We saw and felt this painful reality recently in the disenfranchisement of workers in the central United States and the United Kingdom, where those who were marginalized by the offshoring of manufacturing jobs and the perception of an elite that has lost touch with the needs of the people, influenced with disproportionate power the election of President Trump and Britain's exit from the European Union (Friedman 2016)[79.]

If machines eliminate jobs, and jobs give our lives meaning, what are we going to do to keep ourselves believing that we matter? The answers to this question are myriad and complex, but, fundamentally, the implications are that whether machines do our jobs tomorrow or not, we need somewhere to go and something to do. Work in the form of the jobs we hold benefits us individually and as a society in ways that are not only economic but also essential to our humanity.

How Machines Can Reinforce What Humans Do Best

It's easy to feel threatened by the advent of automation, artificial intelligence, and machines that can do much of what we do better and faster. It's intimidating. When I watched the 2016 movie *Hidden Figures*, I was amazed that human beings once did work that is primarily done today by computers: calculate huge and complex formulas quickly. As wonderful as the advent of computing was for NASA, all those good minds were out of work once the computers were up to speed. So how can machines support what we do best, not threaten it?

By speeding up data calculations, computers increase efficiency and the quality of results, which means that people have more time to think about the implications of whatever results are created. What does this mean? What should we do with this knowledge? The process of considering data and making it meaningful by taking action is uniquely human, and computing helps us do it more often.

The advent of big data means that we know more, by aggregating and comparing data, than ever before. Having a computer gather, store, and compare vast amounts of available information enables sweeping change. Beyond aggregating and comparing consumer data, such as which toothpaste sells more, peppermint or spearmint, analyzing data helps us, as a world-wide community, to see such things as the implications of declining immunization rates on community health or the long-term effect of an extended commute time on productivity.

A second way that technology aids the work of people is by removing the rote and mind-numbing tasks that people hate anyway. Years ago, my sister worked on a speaker manufacturing line. Her job was to put blue and green wires on the back of a box. She did this 800 times daily, and her boss wanted her to do it 1,000. As Jamie said, "Yikes, it was mind-numbing work that didn't invite any of my intelligence or creativity. Moving from 800 to 1,000 didn't feed my soul." Let's leave that work up to machines!

Third, machines and automation allow us to connect more with others across common platforms. When medical records, for example, can be shared across agencies, physicians' decision-making, and thus healthcare, are improved because access to information is instant. Similarly, technology enables collaboration across time zones and geography since people everywhere can see the same data, simultaneously contribute and build on each other's ideas. These technological advances facilitate innovation, education, and collaboration in a wide variety of settings.

A fourth impact on how we work with technology is the advent of blockchain to democratize information, remove profiteers, and ensure data integrity. Decentralizing technology and wrapping information in shared repositories forces us to use the consensus of many to drive decisions rather than the whims of one or a few. While this technology is not yet mainstream, it has the potential to bring out the best we can offer as human beings to make decisions that consider the common good.

AI and machine learning appear to be catapulting us into a future that's vastly different from the way we work today. The possibility of a cataclysmic, Terminator-esque future is just that—one possibility among many. Fortunately, the workers and leaders of today can shape the future of our workplaces.

There's no doubt that we'll work with technology in the future. But what are the implications of that technology on how we work and how we live? What we need right now are leaders who have the courage to ask, over and over, the essential questions that shape our workplaces. In Bravespace workplaces of tomorrow people won't simply be replaced with machines; instead robots, AI, and technology will be leveraged to activate the best possible decision-making and partnerships of the people who work in them.

Endnotes

73 Pew Research Center. 2018. "Mobile Fact Sheet." Pew Research Center: Internet & Technology (February 5). http://www.pewinternet.org/fact-sheet/mobile/.

74 Turing, A. M. 1950. "Computing Machinery and Intelligence." *Mind* 49: 433–60.

75 Turing, A. M. 1937. "On Computable Numbers, with an Application to the Entscheidungsproblem." *Proceedings of the London Mathematical Society* 2, 42 (1), 230–65.

76 Specifically, Turing uses first-order logic to prove that Alonzo Church's lambda-calculus—a system of logic on which any natural function can be computed—was equivalent to his Turing machine. He then uses his Turing machine to prove that there can be no general process for determining whether a given formula written in lambda-calculus is provable. Like I said, this is thick stuff. If you're interested, I recommend Charles Petzold's *The Annotated Turing.*

77 McKinsey Global Institute. 2018. "How Will Automation Affect Jobs, Skills, and Wages?" (March). https://www.mckinsey.com/featured-insights/future-of-work/how-will-automation-affect-jobs-skills-and-wages.

78 Drum, Kevin. 2017. "You Will Lose Your Job to a Robot – and Sooner than You Think." *Mother Jones* (November/December). https://www.motherjones.com/politics/2017/10/you-will-lose-your-job-to-a-robot-and-sooner-than-you-think/.

79 Friedman, George. 2016. "3 Reasons Brits Voted for Brexit," *Forbes* (July 5). https://www.forbes.com/sites/johnmauldin/2016/07/05/3-reasons-brits-voted-for-brexit/#5de9a3f11f9d.

CHAPTER 20

On Profit, Size, and Sharing Wealth

There is no greatness where there is no simplicity,
goodness and truth.

—Leo Tolstoy

When I shifted my career from nonprofit management to the world of business, I did so in part to improve my family's economics. As the primary earner in a dual-income family with two, then three, children, I needed to make more money. Business was an excellent way to do that because the pay was higher and there was more room to grow in responsibility. But I felt conflicted about leaving behind my nonprofit roots. I wondered if, in supporting my family, I had started to contribute to a flawed economic system that potentially damaged others' families. What might I and others have to give up to contribute to a thriving society for all?

Profit Is Not Enough, But There May Be Cause for Hope

As grateful as I am for the benefits I've received working in business, I am at the same time astounded at the impact that the (often singular) focus on profit has on leaders, on the decisions they make, on the people who work for them, on the natural world we share, and on the communities in which businesses operate. Profit cannot continue to be the singular gold standard for companies of tomorrow. Not only are year-over-year profits unsustainable, but profit is losing status as a motivator for workers. Unlike previous generations of workers, Millennials and the generations behind them (Generation Z) care deeply about the "why" of the organization where they work. They hunger to be able to connect the dots between the work they do and the reason their company exists, both locally and globally. Proactive leaders of tomorrow's companies will spend time discussing and sharing the context of everything they do.

Kate Raworth (2017)[80], radical economist and author of Doughnut Economics, says, "[The] fixation on GDP as a nation's primary measure of progress] has been used to justify extreme inequalities of income and wealth coupled with the unprecedented destruction of the living world. For the twenty-first century, a far bigger goal is needed: meeting the human rights of every person within the means of our life-giving planet." It's time for every organization, whatever its size and scope, to profoundly and deeply examine the reason it exists, and to practice, repeatedly, telling that story to every stakeholder in its ecosystem. Doing so will provide the essential currencies for organizations to identify the human talent they require, even as they also leverage technology and automation.

Reform the Systems

A successful society is a progress machine, turning innovations and fortuitous developments into shared advancement. America's machine is broken. Innovations fly at us, but progress eludes us. A thousand world-changing initiatives won't change that. Instead, we must reform the basic systems that allow people to live decently—the systems that decide what kind of school children attend, whether politicians listen to donors or citizens, whether people can tend to their ailments, whether they are paid enough, and with sufficient reliability, to make plans and raise kids. There are a significant number of winners who recognize their role in propping up a bad system. They might be convinced that solving problems for all, at the root, will mean higher taxes, smaller profits, and fewer homes. Changing the world asks more than giving back. It also takes giving something up.

—Anand Giridharadas, *Winners Take All*

There is hope that things are changing for big companies. In its report, *The Rise of the Social Enterprise* (Agarwal et al. 2018)[81], Deloitte argues that there's a tipping point of change for organizations today. Traditional organizations will become social enterprises, which combine revenue growth and profit-making with respect and support of their environments and stakeholder networks. They name the three influencers of this sea change:

- The power of the individual is growing, with Millennials at the forefront.
- Businesses are expected to fill a widening leadership vacuum in society.
- Technological change has unforeseen impacts on society even as it creates massive opportunities to achieve sustainable, inclusive growth.

These trends indicate what tomorrow's leaders must think about to thrive.

If You Win, I Lose Economics

The very economic system I've grown up believing in has gone awry, and the time has come for business to take a more substantial role in fixing it. Oxfam's report citing that the wealthiest 1% of people in the world hold almost 50% of the world's wealth and that they're getting richer is both old news and, at the same time, appalling (Hardoon 2015)[82]. American ethical and economic assumptions have inculcated in me a strong sense of surety that hard work pays off. I've always felt that earning a living for myself (from selling my garden squash by the roadside as a kid to running a thriving consulting firm) would facilitate a lifestyle that worked for me (safety, shelter, healthcare, education for my children, comfort, small luxuries). And as a well-educated, white, middle-aged, able-bodied, heterosexual woman living in twenty-first-century America, I've benefited from great privilege and genuine effort. Along the way, though, the gap between my income and others' has widened in ways that degrade the quality of life for many. It's easy for me to keep making more money for myself and more profit for my clients' companies, but to do so requires disregarding what's happening to the fabric of global society. I cannot, in good conscience, do so. Can you? There's a better way, I believe, that demands of us a direct exploration of our contribution to the common good.

According to Oxfam's 2015 report[83], the world's richest 1% were expected to have as much wealth as the remaining 99% of the world by 2016. To put that another way, the report states that the 80 wealthies people on the planet will have the same wealth as the poorest 3.5 billion people: 80 people's wealth = 3.5 billion people's wealth.

Oxfam's latest research is even more shocking (Pimentel 2018): "Last year (2017) saw the biggest increase in billionaires in history, one more every two days. This huge increase could have ended global extreme poverty seven times over. And 82% of all wealth created in the last year went to the top 1%, and nothing went to the bottom 50%."

Experts speculate that politics and policies that favor big business and the wealthy have exponentially increased disparity between the über rich and the world's poorest. And the mega-tech companies are making things even worse. Nicholas Bloom (2017)84 wrote in Harvard Business Review that "the result of countless strategic decisions in pursuit of [monetary] goals by Google and other elite companies throughout the world—not just in tech—has been to raise the compensation of some workers far more than others." Jamie Bartlett (2017)[85] elaborated in the *Spectator*, arguing that "the meeting of techno-utopianism and profit-making is an unstoppable force, and it has a dark side. One result is that it creates two almost entirely separate worlds." One world is getting richer, richer, and richer. Even though both groups work hard, one is getting poorer, poorer, and poorer. With this wealth disparity come all the problems of people not thriving: poverty, violence, poor health, inequity, and more.

I wonder if we have deluded ourselves into thinking that this is acceptable. That it is perfectly okay that our system creates more and more luxury and excess for a tiny few while the vast majority live with less. Do we believe that these inequalities are created purely by the hard work of the ultra-rich and, by default, tell ourselves a story that the non-rich are simply not working hard enough? In the companies and organizations I work with, everyone usually works hard, including those in lower-wage jobs, such as night shift or unskilled workers. Disproportionate pay to CEOs and shareholders from the wages of employees contributes to these inequities and erodes the meaning of hard work.

Without digging into the complexities of tax law and the policies that have created this situation, let's underline what Winnie Byanyima, Executive Director of Oxfam, said in their report: "It is time our leaders took on the powerful vested interests that stand in the way of a fairer and more prosperous world."

I remember that when I was a kid at school, I was short on lunch some days, and I borrowed from my friends to fill up. And some days, my lunch box was full, and I shared it with them. Metaphorically, it feels wrong to eat a luscious, protein-rich meal while my classmate beside me gets by on stale Cheetos and fake juice. Businesses, whether micro-entities or megaliths that are "too big to fail" must evaluate how they reward excellence and how they share for the common good.

Bravespace workplaces—organizations that know how to share for the common good—will lead tomorrow's work world. Some actions you could take if you seek to make your company fit for human life (a Bravespace workplace) in the context of wealth disparity are:

- Evaluate and understand your pay practices to ensure equity across roles.
- Look at the pay gap between your lowest-paid employee and your CEO and ask yourself if this ratio is appropriate.
- Make courageous change when inequity is found—do the right thing.
- Remember that all jobs in a company make it click—pay your leaders commensurate with their roles and pay the employees who do your dirtiest jobs what they deserve.
- Look for ways to prevent waste inside your company so that there's more funding available for employee compensation, retirement, and benefits.
- Decide how much is enough (there is "enough") for you and your shareholders to make and proactively manage the overage responsibly by reinvesting locally, sharing with employees, reducing prices, and making charitable gifts.
- Notice the gap between your wealthiest employees or shareholders and your poorest and seek strategies with your leaders to reduce the gap.
- Keep your profit local.

- Pay the taxes you and your companies owe—these provide necessary social, law enforcement, judicial, and other services that make our society work for all.

My stomach turns at this wealth disparity. I'm disgusted. I'm proud of my success and have nothing to feel ashamed of (and neither do you). And while ultimately, lawyers and policy makers set the policies that help to make the rich get richer, each of us can and must do more to end the disparity. Winston Churchill said, "Where there is great power, there is great responsibility." Changing the heartbreaking wealth disparity starts with responsible and accountable business owners and shareholders who are making a profit today and have power. It's our job to notice the wealth disparity, to call out its inequity, and to actively and courageously make room for our fellow citizens of the world who also work hard but don't have equal privilege and access.

For our world economy to work, we cannot just turn our heads away from the "other 3.5 billion."

The growth of the global economy reached 3% in 2018, but as the United Nations (Drysdale 2018)[86] says in its most recent report, "Recent improvements in growth remain unevenly distributed across countries and regions. Economic prospects for many commodity exporters remain particularly challenging. Negligible growth in per capita GDP is anticipated in several parts of Africa, Western Asia, Latin America, and the Caribbean. The impacted regions combined are home to 275 million people living in extreme poverty. Without sustained economic growth, the chances of bringing that number to zero remain slim. To achieve the goals of eradicating poverty and creating decent jobs for all, it is essential to address the longer term structural issues that hold back a faster progress towards sustainable development."

A business that expands and benefits some but diminishes and harms others is ultimately good for no one. As noted writer and teacher Meg Wheatley (2002)[87] says, "In a complex system, there is no such thing as simple cause and effect. There's no one person to blame, or to take the credit." It's time for organizations to get back to basics and remember what the people who work for them need and what the world needs.

The Common Good

Bravespace workplaces can and will be used to remedy the ills caused by unhealthy workplaces, wealth disparity, and the dark side of profit as a singular goal. The solutions aren't complex, but they aren't easy. The work requires action from every single employee and leaders especially. I've seen it happen in businesses worldwide, and it's a powerful experience to watch organizations get it right. What it takes is a recognition, acknowledgment, and mindset that we're locally and globally connected. When we do something here, it has an effect there, within organizations, between organizations, and in communities. We are interdependent, and organizations that understand this and operationalize it will become Bravespace workplaces, fit for human life.

My motivation for writing *Bravespace Workplace* comes from my frustration in knowing that we've understood for a long time what work conditions bring out the best in people, yet few companies have built themselves accordingly. I received my graduate degree in the study of people in systems (organizational development) in 1989. And while the theory and practice have incrementally advanced over 30 years, we knew to a great extent then what we know now: human beings are what make organizations great, and when people feel connected, seen, and worthy at work, they perform better. Why can't we get it right after all this time? And why, despite what we know, is the state of work worsening?

The stories of recent workplace failures are significant and dramatic. The #MeToo stories. The fall of Wall Street. Amazon's toxic workplace. Tech's bullying. Nike's gender and wage inequities. The digital age means we can see more into the inner workings of organizations than we could before, and when we look inside many big companies, we feel dirty. How do we know what a sick organization looks like, and yet we can't seem to build many people-centered ones? Stanford University professor Jeffrey Pfeffer (2018)[88] argues in his book, *Dying for a Paycheck* that human sustainability should be as important as environmental stewardship. Pfeffer considers workplaces an environmental hazard, citing data suggesting that unhealthy workplaces are responsible for approximately 125,000 deaths and $130 billion in excess costs in the United States annually. Clearly people at work aren't doing well.

The last 10-plus years of media attention focused on the workplace has made it seem that healthy workplaces are all about the perks: on-site dry cleaning, nap pods, and 24-hour coffee stations. Wild and crazy perks, mainly coming out of Silicon Valley's explosive growth in the tech sector, including arcades, jobs without titles, and unlimited vacation time, which draw our attention to the surface aspects of a company. But what I've repeatedly seen is that what really matters to people are the subtle, internal perks. It seems that the media has been focusing on the wrong things. And the costs of this are grave.

Workplaces that aren't fit for human life accrue staggering costs. Gallup (2013)[89] estimates that actively disengaged employees cost the United States $450 to $550 billion in lost productivity annually. A bad hire costs a company revenue, customers, and productivity, in addition to the hard costs of recruiting, training, and developing a new employee (as much as $50,000 in the United States). The costs increase the longer a misfit employee is on the job.

Companies aren't the only ones paying for disengagement. The costs to individuals are shocking and terrifying. Jeffrey Pfeffer (2018)[90] contends that many modern management commonalities such as long work hours, work-family conflict, and economic insecurity, are toxic to employees, destroying engagement, increasing turnover, and destroying people's physical and emotional health. They are also damaging to company performance. The solution to this horror isn't a workplace wellness program, which Pfeffer sees as a fairly worthless bandage applied to a self-inflicted wound.

Small Companies Provide A Glimmer of Hope

A small but critical caveat: there is some evidence that employees at small companies are doing better. According to Gallup research (2017a)[91], the largest US companies have the lowest levels of engagement, while businesses with fewer than

25 employees have the highest. And in one recent report, 75% of small business workers surveyed said they were "very" or "extremely" satisfied in their role with a small employer. There are many reasons for this, ranging from more flexible work arrangements, employees being able to see their impact, and non-cash incentives.

There's something important to learn from this research: leaders' ability to directly influence things within their control is much greater in small companies. The work that my colleagues and I have done with these smaller companies enabled their leaders to facilitate change more swiftly and with more lasting impact.

Endnotes

80 Raworth, Kate. 2017. *Doughnut Economics.* New York: Random House Business.

81 Agarwal, Dimple, Josh Bersin, Gaurav Lahiri, Jeff Schwartz, and Erica Volini. 2018. *Deloitte Insights: The Rise of the Social Enterprise.* https://www2.deloitte.com/content/dam/insights/ us/articles/ HCTrends2018/2018-HCtrends_Rise-of-the-social-enterprise.pdf.

82 Hardoon, Deborah. 2015. *Wealth: Having It All and Wanting More.*

83 Oxfam Issue Briefing (January). https://d1tn3vj7xz9fdh. cloudfront.net/s3fs-public/file_attachments/ib-wealth-having-all-wanting-more-190115-en.pdf

84 Bloom, Nicholas. 2017. "Corporations in the Age of Inequality." *Harvard Business Review* (March 21). https://hbr.org/2017/03/ corporations-in-the-age-of-inequality.

85 Bartlett, Jamie. 2017. "Silicon Valley's Wealthy Elite Have Made Social Inequality Worse." *The Spectator* (August 12). https:// www. spectator.co.uk/2017/08/silicon-valleys-wealthy-elite-have-made-social-inequality-worse/.

86 Drysdale, Carla, ed. 2018. World Economic Situation and Prospects 2018. United Nations. https://www.un.org/ development/desa/dpad/wp-content/uploads/sites/45/ publication/WESP2018_Full_ Web-1.pdf.

87 Wheatley, Margaret J. 2002. "It's an Interconnected World," *Shambhala Sun* (April). https://margaretwheatley.com/articles/ interconnected.html.

88 Pfeffer, Jeffrey. 2018. *Dying for a Paycheck.* New York: Harper Collins

89 Gallup. 2013. *State of the American Workplace: Employee Engagement Insights for U.S. Business Leaders.* https://www. gallup.com/ services/176708/state-american-workplace.aspx.

90 Pfeffer, Jeffrey. 2018. *Dying for a Paycheck.* New York: Harper Collins.

91 Gallup. 2017a. *State of the American Workplace.* https://www. gallup. com/workplace/238085/state-american-workplace-report-2017. aspx.

PART VII

Get Going

CHAPTER 21

Begin with You

Great projects start out feeling like buildings.
There are architects, materials, staff, rigid timelines, permits,
engineers, a structure. It works or it doesn't. Build something
that doesn't fall down. On time.

But in fact, great projects, like great careers and relationships
that last, are gardens. They are tended, they shift, they grow.
They endure over time, gaining a personality and reflecting
their environment. When something dies or fades away,
we prune, replant and grow again.

Perfection and polish aren't nearly as important as good light,
good drainage and a passionate gardener.

By all means, build. But don't finish. Don't walk away.

Here we grow.

—Seth Godin

Now that the idea of Bravespace workplaces has been introduced and defined, it's time to get started on the specific actions you can take using the tools we've covered so far.

Let's look at a CEO with whom I recently worked. He was struggling with the internal dynamics of his company despite incredibly fast financial success. His employees were feeling tired and burned out. His leadership team needed to step away from the details to focus on the future, but they didn't know how. He had two senior leaders whom employees feared. He was worried about the toll on his marriage and home life. I told him that I thought I could help.

"Great," he said. "Will it be complex?"

"Nope, not complex," I said, "but not easy either."

It can be hard to know where to start when creating a workplace that truly brings out the best in everyone who works there. In my 30-plus years of experience consulting with companies of all types, here are the top ten behaviors to start with:

1. **Adopt a people-centered mindset.** Spend time getting your head behind the notion that your company's greatness depends on the people in it. Being people-centered doesn't mean your company exists so that your people can be happy; it means designing your workspace—the physical and felt environment of your organization—to encourage people to thrive. Thriving people bring all their talents to benefit your company.

2. **Bring flexibility to your approach.** There's no one right way to create a Bravespace workplace. Your way will be unique to you and will depend on the nature of your business, your style of leading, and the special alchemy of your workforce. Be flexible with what others have tried, and don't be afraid to customize your approach based on your

values and priorities. Stick with what we know people need from work and stay focused on fulfilling those needs.

3. **Involve others.** Leaders in the best companies I've worked with take the time and effort to get input and ideas from everyone there. This doesn't mean that they make decisions by consensus, the tediousness of which can grind productivity to a crawl, but rather that leaders at all levels prioritize asking people what they think, listening to their responses, and communicating openly and freely in both directions. Open involvement increases buy-in, which increases participation, which increases ownership. Genuine involvement makes everyone in your organization accountable, not just you.

4. **See the benefit beyond.** Your top priority will remain the efficacy and performance of your company but remember that your company's profit depends on its overall health. The presence of your organization should enhance the communities in which you operate, the environment in which you operate and the resources you use should be responsibly cared for, and the people who work for you should feel that they're better people as a result of working for your organization. Consciously choose to see beyond profit to other indicators that your company is doing well.

5. **Address leaders first.** Every employee at every level knows the company through their direct manager. Period. This means that even if you're the best CEO, general manager, executive director, or business owner in the history of the world if one of your leaders is a tyrant, an abuser, or

just a negative influence, your employees will not thrive. In Bravespace workplaces, time, energy, resources, and conversation are invested in the art and science of leading well. Nothing matters more. Leadership is not for the faint of heart, and advanced degrees and years of experience don't necessarily make a great leader. Know when you have a great leader who inspires loyalty, fosters esteem, and brings out the best in your people. Develop those leaders and keep them.

6. **Remember that life is work.** We work for many reasons, but no matter our motivations, our work is part of our lives. It matters to us, and it impacts our human development, our view of the world, and our ability to thrive at home and in our communities. Your employees lives outside of work shape and define the life they bring to work, so don't pretend there's a wall between the two. The people, activities, and circumstances your employees encounter away from your workplace are essential to what they bring into the workspace, so talk to them about those things.

7. **Start with small changes.** It doesn't take a radical change to have a positive impact and bring your company closer to becoming a Bravespace workplace. There's no need for a wholesale makeover or herculean consulting resources. Start somewhere, anywhere, and keep at it. Small changes have a massive impact on the way your employees experience your organization. Small, effective changes are far preferable to big, romantic, programmatic changes that will fail for lack of bandwidth.

8. **Listen to understand.** Having almost finished reading *When Work is Good*, you may know where to start and what to do. Good for you! Go out and talk to people in your organization about your ideas and hear what they think. Really listen. As the owner, CEO, general manager, or executive director, it's difficult for you to see your organization neutrally: your position limits your perspective. When you listen to your leaders, front-line employees, and customers, you add nuance, detail, and clarity to your ideas about what to do.

9. **Align head and heart.** Remember emotion is part of your brain, too, and your emotional states are a powerful source of information to help you and others make decisions and lead. Whether you have an MBA, 30 years in your industry, or just a killer technology to bring to market, focus on your heart skills. Doing so will grow your capacity to engage with others, create meaningful connection, and inspire followership more than anything else you might try. We are drawn to vulnerability in others, so bravely show up.

10. **Walk your talk.** People working for you will read the memos, attend the all-hands meetings, and adhere to the policies. But more than anything else, they'll watch and absorb what you, and the leaders you hire, do daily. Everything—from how you run a meeting to what hours you work—communicates information to your employees about what you value. This, in turn, shapes their point of view about whether your company is one in which they can learn, grow, and thrive. Make your actions conscious,

ask about the impact you have and do what you say you will do. Your employees are watching.

Making work good is all about bringing out the absolute best in the human beings who work in them, despite our imperfect and complex human motivations, habits, needs, and issues. Bravespace workplaces are people-centered because their leaders deeply understand people who make all the positive things happen at work. If you want your company to become a Bravespace workplace, start at any of the elements we've looked at in this book. Start with courage, because even when you don't know the answer, there is a way forward. Start with heart, because it's what draws people to you and your company. Start with faith, because while you, too, are imperfect, you want to lead your organization, and what you do matters.

Just start.

CHAPTER 22

A Manifesto for
When Work is Good

The world of work was broken long before the global pandemic.

If you go back far enough in time, you'll discover a world ignorant even of the word "work."

Life and the things people did were all one.

People created—baskets, stools, crops, and wheat—but the idea of labor as a measurable commodity didn't exist.

Over time, people recognized that the activity of "doing things" was unique enough to be signaled out against other words. Thus, came leisure.

The moment when work became a concept changed human lives immeasurably. Alongside it came the notions of earning one's leisure time or altering social status (and comfort) through effort.

People found and sought out others doing similar work to themselves to create specialized communities of workers.

Even without the great items and services produced by a working world, the world improved when people started to "work."

Parallel to its glorious wonders, though, work revealed its blunders.

As people exchanged their labor for money, humans stopped seeing each other as neighbors and relationships became about what we each produce.

Work began to drive a wedge between people and their lives.

Fathers went weeks without connecting with their children.

Grueling hours and sometimes physical danger extracted a huge toll on people's health.

Autonomy decreased and as a result, so did engagement and purpose for workers.

In and of themselves, these blunders aren't the fault of work. They're caused by the failure of work to meet our basic needs.

You see, from that time to now, our basic human needs haven't changed. Of course, we don't get these met only from work, but work plays a huge role in the overall quality of our lives.

Our world needs work; let's build workplaces to meet people's needs.

More than ever in recent memory, now is an apt moment to reimagine work.

Across the board, workplaces have been disturbed by the COVID-19 pandemic.

Our systems are broken, our people are tired.

Let's leverage this pause to start fresh and build a better working world than before.

As guidance and motivation, I propose the following Work Manifesto for employers to hold up high in their commitment to treating their workers with the respect every human deserves.

Work: The New Manifesto

- People make organizations great. Period.
- When people thrive at work, they are better outside of work—they're happier, more resilient, and contribute to strong communities.
- Organizations get better results when the people in them are connected, engaged, and feel they belong.
- The workplace is not a place; it's a community—one where interdependence is the default.
- All face-to-face, in-person time is precious and should be designed to generate meaningful connections.
- Communities of true belonging notice, name, and interrupt the mindsets, patterns, processes, and systems that disproportionately benefit some over others.

- Each workplace is unique. Leaders must discover what is best for their organization by asking the right questions and being willing to really hear the answers.
- Leaders who are good for people matter. It's time for toxic leaders to go.
- Flexibility is a central perk for humans at work. Working communities that build flexibility into how they do things will attract the best talent.
- People benefit from knowing why the work they do matters in the world.
- Pay must cover basic human necessities in every role from the bottom to the top.

People Leadership, Conscious and Brave Culture, and Teams Who Care are the levers that help people thrive at work. Brave leaders must challenge the assumptions about what works at work and craft sustainable, new ways of getting work done that treat humans as humans.

When this happens, people will bring their highest and best to work. Results will soar, families and communities will be healthier, and everybody wins.

Epilogue

I can practically taste what it would be like if every employer decided to make work good. I've seen enough organizations achieve it that I know in my bones that it's possible. I am motivated by my deep-seated hope for my children and yours that we, the business owners, the leaders, and the entrepreneurs, will foster a quiet but potent revolution that turns the tide of job misery once and for all.

When this happens, people will work with energy and optimism, not every day, but most days. Work, at all stages of life, will be viewed as central to our well-being, as important as rest and health, instead of simply as the drudgery we face on the road to retirement. Through work, we'll achieve meaning because we know the impact of our effort. At work, people will find critical connections with other human beings, connections that reduce their isolation and loneliness.

Work will no longer erode and suffocate the health of our beloved families and friends because we're overwhelmed and overworked. Instead, work will enliven and enrich families of all types. Everyone will feel free to make choices supporting their families, whether taking leave after a child is born or adopted, caring for elders, working flexible hours, or having virtual meetings. Organizations will include insider groups and outsider groups at all levels so that across the identifiers of race, gender, sexual orientation, and more, there will be equity and inclusion. Men and women will make equal pay for equal work.

Work will be where mistakes happen on the road to learning and where shame is replaced by compassion and worthiness. At work, we'll play sometimes, and value rest as essential to productivity. Hard conversations will happen in the Bravespace workplaces of tomorrow, driven by the belief that conflict is essential to partnership, and we'll be both clear and kind.

Leaders of tomorrow who make work good will show up, be honest, and lead by example and integrity. They'll model the common values and vision that benefit all employees so that we remember why we do what we do and how we want to work together.

Bravespace workplaces of tomorrow will be profitable, but not at the expense of the environment or the communities in which they operate.

With the knowledge that people are what make companies great, Bravespace workplaces of tomorrow will be healthy and safe places for people to co-exist. In these places, our children, and theirs, will be able to bring their gifts, ideas, talent, wisdom, and experience forward even as they bring quirks, imperfections, and needs. They'll be welcomed whether they are insiders or outsiders, for their talents and gifts, for the ways they're different, and for the ways they are the same.

When work is good, it will be where we go to activate, enliven, and tenderly support the complicated humans that we are so that we can bring all of ourselves to work every day. It will be a place where we create great things together, learn, connect, and contribute.

Index

About the Author

Organizations large and small are routinely brought to their knees by the so-called "soft stuff" of people problems–as anyone knows who has tried, this work is hard. As a facilitator, protagonist, consultant, entrepreneur, author, employer, and relentless optimist, Moe Carrick believes that people can and should thrive at work, and that when they do, organizations succeed. With over 30 years of work in organizations on issues of partnership, leadership, inclusion, strategy and culture, Moe drives home that rigorous self-awareness, courage, honest dialogue, active involvement, and empathy are fundamentals to building full partnerships based on trust and curiosity. Moe is Founder of Moementum, Inc. and holds a Master's Degree in Organizational Development, working with organizations in all sectors to grow healthy cultures and leaders who are good for people. She is author of other two bestselling books, *FIT Matters: How to Love Your Job* and *Bravespace Workplace: Making Your Company Fit for Human Life.* Moe publishes a weekly Blog and hosts the podcast, *Let's Make Work Human.*

"Most businesses today are draining the life out of their most essential assets: their workers. Moe Carrick is helping us change this toxic paradigm. Warm, witty, and data-driven, Carrick unflinchingly tackles the false dichotomy that a company must choose between profit and people. She shows us how to transform our workplace into a culture that brings out the best in our people. I am grateful for the opportunity to use Carrick's refreshing and practical Bravespace model with my team."

—**Glennon Doyle,** author of the #1 *New York Times* bestseller *Love Warrior* and founder of Together Rising

"We all know it: people *are* what make companies great and Carrick breaks right through the bull to get real with what it takes to make every workplace a bravespace. If you want your people to bring their best every day—*read this book now!*"

—**Marshall Goldsmith,** #1 *New York Times* bestselling author of *Triggers, MOJO,* and *What Got You Here Won't Get You There.*

"Today, more than ever, effective leadership requires more than just the head, but the heart. In this book, Moe Carrick outlines how leaders can strengthen their organizations through caring, connecting, and cultivating healthy cultures. This is a must-read for leaders who want their people, and their organizations, to thrive."

—**Ron Fritz,** CEO, Tech Soft 3D

"This is a must-read for today's leaders: When a workplace is toxic, then the employee's energy is spent 'coping,' with great cost in their happiness, health, and creativity. And there is great loss to the organization: through lost opportunity. Moe Carrick shows how to diagnose key toxic issues and how to engage to create an organization where 'humans can show up as they are.' Performance will soar!"

—**Rod Ray,** Ph.D., PE, founder, and former CEO,
Bend Research

"Early on, we realized that culture is an enduring competitive advantage, and our people have been key to Hydro Flask's success ever since. This book offers inspiration and practical tools for any employer who wants to win both by doing what is best for their people and subsequently winning the war for talent."

—**Scott Allan,** former SVP. CEO, and
General Manager, Hydro Flask

"Moe Carrick does it again—her book is a must-read, especially for people leaders. Moe's lifelong work of studying work cultures and human performance are illuminated in her book. She has spent several decades studying how humans need a sense of purpose, to be seen, valued, and nurtured. She has witnessed, time and again, companies who foster cultures where these important dimensions exist, see it in both the bottom-line results of their organizations and in how customers are taken care of. She provides practical methods to chart your journey to enriching the lives of others and yourself along the way. A worthwhile read!"

—**Michelle Clemens,** past Vice President of Human
Resources, Seattle University, REI, and more

"In business? Then you're in the 'people business.' And if you're not creating, growing, and leading a Bravespace Workplace, you're at risk. This book is the instruction manual you've been waiting for!"

—**David Taylor-Klaus,** PCC, CPCC, CTPC, CC-IQC, founder of DTK Coaching

"Moe captures a poignant message that has never been more important for our humanity and the future of work: How do we bring our best whole-selves to every part of our lives— including work where we spend most of our waking hours? Her transparent and vulnerable voice is easy to read, easy to love and an *inspiring* call to action for all stakeholders in the global economy. A must-read for aspiring world-changers like me bucking the status quo!"

—**Shannon Keith,** CEO and Founder of Sudara

"*When Work is Good* offers practical tools and necessary inspiration for leaders to create an environment where their people can thrive, be joyful, and feel that their opinions and contributions matter."

—**Marc Hoffman,** Partner, A.T. Kearney

"It seems so simple, remembering to lead with heart. Moe Carrick's book gave me thoughtful questions on how to lead to ensure our business is people and planet first."

—**Casey Hanisko,** past President, ATTA / Adventure 360

"A company's biggest asset is its human capital. So why do so many squander it with one-size-fits-all policies and neglectful practices? Creating a worker-centered workplace is not only the right thing to do; it's good business. And this book is your blueprint, a must for every leader and manager."

—**Norie Quintos,** principal at Norie Quintos Media and editor at large at *National Geographic Traveler*

"This book provides practical, easy-to-implement tools to do right by those in your workplace, and in doing so, to ensure that your business does well, and the world does better. Thank you Moe Carrick!"

—**Mara Rudman,** JD, Senior VP Policy/Projects, Business Executives for National Security; former Deputy Assistant to the President, National Security Council

"Business owners and CEOs are still designing workplaces and company cultures in antiquated ways. It's no surprise that the youth of today are shying away from corporate jobs, even vilifying them. They simply leave no space for individuality and they don't ask themselves often enough, what can we do for our people. This book is a daring and refreshing manuscript on how to break this mold and re-invent company culture. We should all be inspired going to work every day and we should feel that the places we work are extensions of our value system. After all, we can accomplish so much more working together."

—**Omar Samra,** CEO, adventurer, and UN Goodwill Ambassador

"I am a firm believer that companies can win doing the right thing for the customer, employee, and shareholder. Too often companies favor the latter and the employee suffers the most. Moe offers a great handbook for managers to use to create a work environment for their teams to thrive and change the current paradigm."

—**Libby Unger,** Managing Director, Lumineau

"This is a book about how to disrupt how we think about work and work environments. Through an engaging, actionable blend of research and experience, Moe Carrick's latest book provides the vision and tools to create whole-hearted work environments where we all can succeed. A practical, insightful guide for courageous leaders everywhere!"

—**Katie Kilty,** EdD, Principal, MindPower Resources

"There are now three billion working people on this planet. Forty percent report being happy, and thirteen percent are engaged at work. Highly diverse and inclusive workforces that are managed well, capture 46 to 58 percent higher financial performance. Being people-centric, this book points out the way to make your people more happy and engaged."

—**Karen Brown,** Founder/Managing Director/Consultant, Bridge Arrow

"For anyone who has ever worked in a toxic environment and who says "Never again!" to that—read and share this book. We would have a happier and more fulfilled society if this was required reading (and enacting) for every business owner or CEO."

—**Daniela Papi-Thornton,** CEO, Systems-led Leadership

"Every business professional will benefit from this essential reading (on work in the 21st century). Moe Carrick will inspire you to rethink everything you thought you knew about the workplace and provides honest, clear-eyed, and healing recommendations for our best work lives."

—**Laura Wendt,** Ph.D., neuroscientist, international speaker, and Manager, Global Diversity and Inclusion, at A.T. Kearney

"As a pioneering organization operating in two post-conflict countries with staff from many different ethnic backgrounds, we have faced many challenges working together. Moe Carrick offers a roadmap for leaders everywhere for what really matters in their roles.

—**Praveen Moman,** Founder, and CEO,
Volcanoes Safaris (Uganda/Rwanda)

"In today's healthcare environment, creating a brave, transparent workplace is an amazing opportunity to counteract the impact of the complexity and uncertainty that underlies the current system."

—**Megan Haase,** FNP, CEO Mosaic Medical